PRENTICE HALL MATHEMATICS

COURSE 1

Progress Monitoring Assessments

PEARSON

Prentice
Hall

Boston, Massachusetts
Upper Saddle River, New Jersey

Pearson Prentice Hall™ is a trademark of Pearson Education, Inc.
Pearson® is a registered trademark of Pearson plc.
Prentice Hall® is a registered trademark of Pearson Education, Inc.

ISBN 0-13-201460-2

2 3 4 5 6 7 8 9 10   10 09 08 07

Table of Contents

About This Book v

Screening Test 1

Benchmark Tests

Benchmark Test 1 7

Benchmark Test 2 13

Benchmark Test 3 19

Benchmark Test 4 25

Benchmark Test 5 31

Quarter 1 Test, Chapters 1–3

• Form A: Regular 39

• Form B: Regular 41

• Form D: Below Level ⬚ 43

• Form E: Below Level ⬚ 45

Quarter 2 Test, Chapters 4–6

• Form A: Regular 47

• Form B: Regular 49

• Form D: Below Level ⬚ 51

• Form E: Below Level ⬚ 53

Quarter 3 Test, Chapters 7–9

• Form A: Regular 55

• Form B: Regular 57

• Form D: Below Level ⬚ 59

• Form E: Below Level ⬚ 61

Quarter 4 Test, Chapters 10–12

• Form A: Regular 63

• Form B: Regular 65

• Form D: Below Level ⬚ 67

• Form E: Below Level ⬚ 69

Mid-Course Test, Chapters 1–6

- Form A: Regular 71
- Form B: Regular 75
- Form D: Below Level L2 79
- Form E: Below Level L2 83

Final Test, Chapters 1–12

- Form A: Regular 87
- Form B: Regular 91
- Form D: Below Level L2 95
- Form E: Below Level L2 99

Test-Taking Strategies 103

Standardized Test Practice

NAEP Practice Test 115

SAT 10 Practice Test 129

ITBS Practice Test 143

TerraNova Practice Test 151

Reports

Screening Test Report 165

Benchmark Test 1 Report 167

Benchmark Test 2 Report 169

Benchmark Test 3 Report 171

Benchmark Test 4 Report 173

Benchmark Test 5 Report 175

Correlation Charts 177

Answers 189

Student Answer Sheets 199

To the Teacher:

During the school year, you assess how students are learning in your classroom using various types of assessments. Prentice Hall's *Progress Monitoring Assessments* provides a clear path to adequate yearly progress through systematic testing and recommendations for remediation.

Formative Assessments

When you give tests that help you identify students' strengths and weaknesses, your assessments are considered formative assessments. The results of these tests serve as a guide in planning and adjusting curriculum to assist struggling students and enhance all students' learning. There are several assessments and related activities in this book to assist you.

Screening Test

Before launching into the curriculum, you need to know how well your students read and how proficient they are in basic computation and problem-solving skills. Use the Screening Test to measure student readiness for your course.

Benchmark Tests

Proficiency testing is at the heart of progress monitoring and student achievement. At specified intervals throughout the year, give Benchmark Tests to evaluate student progress toward mastery of essential content.

Test-Taking Strategies Practice

Since a critical factor of assessment is to provide opportunities for students to learn better, use the Test-Taking Strategies Practice pages to investigate problem-solving strategies and strengthen students' application of these strategies with problems of varying complexity.

Standardized Test Practice

Since the NAEP, SAT 10, ITBS, and TerraNova tests are common assessments at high school, use these pages to acquaint students with topics, question formats, and practice. The activities and practice provided on these pages will allow students to be less anxious when they take these high stakes assessments for evaluation purposes.

Summative Assessments

When you give tests, usually at the end of a quarter or year, and the goal of the assessment is to evaluate mastery, your assessments are considered summative assessments. There are several assessments and related activities in this book to assist you. Quarter Tests, Mid-Course Tests, and Final Tests are available at two levels. The regular levels are designed to measure mastery of content over a span of chapters with the rigor presented in the lessons and exercises of the Student Edition. The below level forms are provided to support less-proficient readers, beginning English-language learners, and other struggling students. The problems meet the same mastery of content, but contain more visual support and fewer problems.

Assessment Support

Providing clear and supportive feedback to students is critical to progress monitoring, so use the comprehensive reports and answer keys provided in this book to map student results and follow-up with relevant remediation assignments.

Screening Test

1. What is the value of the digit 4 in the following number?

   14,032

   A ones

   B tens

   C hundreds

   D thousands

2. Which fraction is modeled by the shaded area below?

   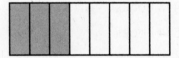

   A $\frac{3}{8}$

   B $\frac{3}{5}$

   C $\frac{5}{8}$

   D $\frac{8}{3}$

3. Which set of decimals is in order from least to greatest?

   A 4.23, 4.12, 4.1, 4.09

   B 4.23, 4.09, 4.1, 4.12

   C 4.09, 4.1, 4.12, 4.23

   D 4.1, 4.12, 4.23, 4.09

4. Of all of the puppies for sale, $\frac{7}{12}$ have white paws. Which statement *best* represents this fact?

   A None of the puppies for sale have white paws.

   B About $\frac{1}{4}$ of the puppies for sale have white paws.

   C About $\frac{1}{2}$ of the puppies for sale have white paws.

   D All of the puppies for sale have white paws.

5. Add.

   584 + 487

   A 961

   B 1,017

   C 1,061

   D 1,071

6. Subtract.

   $$\begin{array}{r} 1,985 \\ -\ 697 \\ \hline \end{array}$$

   A 1,288

   B 1,298

   C 1,312

   D 1,382

7. Add.

$$\frac{2}{9} + \frac{5}{9}$$

A $\frac{7}{18}$

B $\frac{5}{18}$

C $\frac{7}{9}$

D $\frac{11}{14}$

8. Harry sawed $4\frac{3}{4}$ inches off a $6\frac{1}{4}$ inch board. How much board was left?

A $1\frac{1}{4}$ inches

B $1\frac{1}{2}$ inches

C $2\frac{1}{4}$ inches

D $2\frac{1}{2}$ inches

9. Ben had $61.65. He earned $31.50 for picking up walnuts from his neighbor's yard. How much money does Ben have now?

A $92.15

B $92.85

C $93.15

D $93.85

10. Jenna ran a 100-meter race in 14.76 seconds. Kylie ran the same race in 16.03 seconds. How much faster did Jenna run the race than Kylie?

A 1.17 seconds

B 1.27 seconds

C 2.17 seconds

D 2.27 seconds

11. Kim has 8 boxes filled with paperback books. Each box can hold 68 books. How many books does she have in all?

A 76 books

B 448 books

C 544 books

D 608 books

12. Divide.

339 ÷ 3

A 103

B 113

C 123

D 139

13. There are 246 seats in an auditorium. The auditorium is divided into 3 equal sections. How many seats are in each section?

A 62 seats

B 72 seats

C 82 seats

D 92 seats

14. A gardener planted 8 rose bushes, 18 lilies, 10 irises and 24 petunias around the perimeter of a swimming pool. What is the ratio of the number of rose bushes to the number of petunias in the garden?

   A 1 to 3

   B 4 to 9

   C 5 to 12

   D 3 to 4

15. Which number is *not* an odd number?

   A 253

   B 325

   C 352

   D 523

16. Which number is a factor of 412?

   A 32

   B 91

   C 103

   D 113

17. Which statement does *not* form an equation?

   A $54 \times 1 = 54$

   B $54 + 0 = 54$

   C $54 \times 0 = 54$

   D $54 + 1 = 55$

18. Which of the following is *best* measured in terms of capacity?

   A an eyelash

   B juice in a glass

   C a trip to the store

   D a math book on a table

19. James and June both swim 2 miles a day. Which measuring tool should be used to determine the swimmer with the fastest time?

   A a scale

   B a clock

   C a meter stick

   D a thermometer

20. The perimeter P of a square may be found using the formula $P = 4s$, where s is the length of each side. The area of a square may be found using the formula $A = s^2$.

A square has an area of 64 square feet. What is the perimeter of the square?

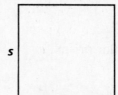

   A 16 feet

   B 32 feet

   C 64 feet

   D 128 feet

21. Use the formula $A = l \times w$ to find the area of the rectangle below.

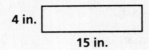

4 in.

15 in.

   A 38 square inches

   B 60 square inches

   C 76 square inches

   D 108 square inches

22. A poster lists the average masses of common objects. Which mass would most likely be given in kilograms?

   A a paperclip

   B a dragonfly

   C a young child

   D a newborn kitten

23. A cereal box is a real-world example of which solid shape?

   A cube

   B sphere

   C rectangle

   D rectangular prism

24. Which geometric figure below is a pentagon?

A   **C**

B   **D**

25. Which statement about triangles is true?

   A The angles in a triangle must equal 180°.

   B A triangle must have at least 1 obtuse angle.

   C The sides in a right triangle are always the same length.

   D The angles in an isosceles triangle are equal.

26. Which solid shape can be formed by the following plane shapes?

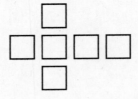

   A cube

   B square pyramid

   C triangular prism

   D rectangular pyramid

27. Which two-dimensional shape(s) are used to make the faces of the solid figure below?

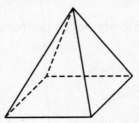

   A rectangles

   B triangles

   C rectangles and squares

   D squares and triangles

28. What type of data display is shown below?

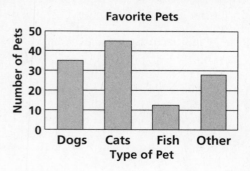

Favorite Pets

A table

B bar graph

C line graph

D frequency table

29. On which activity did Mark spend the most time?

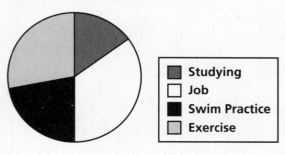

Time Spent on After-School Activities

- Studying
- Job
- Swim Practice
- Exercise

A Job

B Exercise

C Studying

D Swim Practice

30. Which of the following events is certain to occur?

A The sun will set in the west.

B A coin is tossed and it lands on tails.

C It will rain every time you have a party.

D Your best friend scores the winning touchdown.

31. There are 20 marbles in a box: 6 blue marbles, 4 red marbles, 7 green marbles, and 3 black marbles. If you reach into the box and choose one marble, which color of marble are you most likely to pick?

A red

B blue

C black

D green

32. What is the next number in the pattern?

3, 6, 9, 12, …

A 14

B 15

C 18

D 21

33. Solve.

$x + 16 = 42$

A $x = 26$

B $x = 36$

C $x = 58$

D $x = 68$

34. An accountant drives 50 miles a day to work. Which expression represents the total number of miles he drives after x days?

A $50x$

B $50 \div x$

C $x - 50$

D $x + 50x$

35. Which point represents the ordered pair $(1, 3)$?

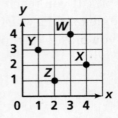

A W

B X

C Y

D Z

36. Samuel has been playing the piano 5 years longer than Marisa. Marisa has been playing for y years. Which equation can be used to find the number of years Marisa has been playing the piano if Samuel has been playing for 13 years?

A $13 = \dfrac{y}{5}$

B $13 = 5y$

C $13 = y + 5$

D $13 = y - 5$

STOP

Benchmark Test 1

1. Estimate. Round each number first.
   38 + 11 + 129

   A 160

   B 170

   C 180

   D 190

2. Estimate using compatible numbers.
   306 × 19

   F 600

   G 3,000

   H 6,000

   J 10,000

3. Estimate using compatible numbers.
   211 ÷ 27

   A 4

   B 8

   C 10

   D 12

4. Write the number five hundred fifty-eight million, two hundred thousand.

   F 500,582,000

   G 558,020,000

   H 500,058,200

   J 558,200,000

5. What is the value of the digit 2 in the number 4.0725?

   A 2 tenths

   B 2 hundredths

   C 2 thousandths

   D 2 ten-thousandths

6. How is the decimal 2.016 expressed in words?

   F two and sixteen thousandths

   G two and sixteen hundredths

   H two and sixteen tenths

   J two and sixteenths

7. The table below shows the population of different cities in Texas. Which answer choice shows the cities with the largest and smallest populations, in that order?

City	Population
Dallas	1,188,580
Austin	656,562
Denton	80,537
Garden Ridge	2,366

   A Garden Ridge, Dallas

   B Austin, Denton

   C Dallas, Austin

   D Dallas, Garden Ridge

8. Which set of decimals is ordered from least to greatest?

 F 2.67, 2.71, 2.99, 2.02

 G 2.99, 2.67, 2.71, 2.02

 H 2.02, 2.67, 2.71, 2.99

 J 2.71, 2.02, 2.99, 2.67

9. Which of the following statements is true?

 A $1.971 > 1.97$

 B $2.53 < 2.3$

 C $4.825 > 4.85$

 D $6.74 < 6.740$

10. Which property is used to make the following statement?

 $$16 + (4 + 10) = (16 + 4) + 10$$

 F Commutative Property of Addition

 G Associative Property of Addition

 H Identity Property of Addition

 J Commutative Property of Multiplication

11. Which of the following is an example of the Identity Property of Multiplication?

 A $13 + 0 = 13$

 B $13 \times 2 = 2 \times 13$

 C $13 \times 1 = 13$

 D $(13 \times 2) \times 4 = (4 \times 13) \times 2$

12. Which of the following is not true?

 F $2 \times 1 = 2$

 G $6 \times 3 \times 9 = 6 \times 9 \times 3$

 H $(5 \times 2) + 3 = 2 + (3 \times 5)$

 J $(5 + 1) + 2 = 1 + (2 + 5)$

13. Which step should be done first when simplifying the following expression?

 $$2 \times 16 - 4 + 5 \times (4 \div 2)$$

 A Add 4 to 5.

 B Subtract 4 from 16.

 C Multiply 5 by 4.

 D Divide 4 by 2.

14. What is the value of the following expression?

 $$(10 + 6) \div 2 + 6 \times 2$$

 F 4

 G 20

 H 28

 J 38

15. Janice has a coupon for \$5.00 off her total purchase at a bookstore. She purchases 4 books priced at \$7.99 each. Which expression represents the total amount Janice spends?

 A $(\$7.99 \times 4) - \$5.00$

 B $(\$7.99 - \$5.00) \times 4$

 C $\$7.99 \times (4 - \$5.00)$

 D $\$7.99 - (\$5.00 \times 4)$

16. Which addition problem is modeled below?

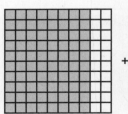 +

 F $8 + 3 = 11$

 G $0.8 + 3 = 3.8$

 H $0.8 + 0.3 = 1.1$

 J $0.08 + 0.3 = 0.38$

17. Find the sum.

$$4.038 + 5.4 + 2.17$$

A 11.08

B 11.18

C 11.590

D 11.608

18. At a concert booth, T-shirts sell for $14.75, posters sell for $8.80, and CDs sell for $12.95. What is the total cost to buy one of each?

F $24.40

G $28.58

H $35.40

J $36.50

19. Find the product.

$$263(4.5)$$

A 1,052.5

B 1,183

C 1,183.5

D 1,315

20. Find the quotient.

$$1.2 \div 0.3$$

F 0.25

G 0.4

H 2.5

J 4.0

21. Kim has a piece of fabric that is 136.5 centimeters long. She cuts the fabric into 6 strips of equal length. How long is each strip?

A 22.25 centimeters

B 22.75 centimeters

C 23.50 centimeters

D 23.75 centimeters

22. What is the mean of the following set of data?

$$3.1, 6.2, 6.1, 5.3, 4.2, 8.1$$

F 5.0

G 5.3

H 5.5

J 5.8

23. Nathan measured the heights of 8 sunflower seedlings. The heights in inches are listed below.

$$4, 4\frac{1}{2}, 5\frac{1}{4}, 5, 5\frac{3}{4}, 3\frac{1}{2}, 5, 4\frac{1}{4}$$

What is the median height of the sunflower seedlings?

A $4\frac{1}{8}$ inches

B $4\frac{3}{4}$ inches

C 5 inches

D $5\frac{3}{8}$ inches

24. A real estate agency sold 5 homes in the past week. The prices of the homes are listed below.

$135,000; $141,000; $138,000; $154,000; $131,000

Which statement most accurately describes the prices of these homes?

F The mean price is less than $138,000.

G The median price is greater than $138,000.

H The median price is less than the mean price.

J The range of the prices is greater than the median price.

25. The ages of musicians in the local symphony are shown in the stem-and-leaf plot below. How many musicians are 40 years old or younger?

Ages of Musicians

```
2 | 2 2 5 7 8 8
3 | 0 3 3 5 6
4 | 0 1 5 7
5 | 2 3 4 5 6
6 | 0 1
```

Key: 2|0 means 20 years old

A 1

B 11

C 12

D 15

26. Each contestant in a game show was given 10 questions to answer. The line plot below shows how many questions each contestant answered correctly. How many contestants got at least half of the questions correct?

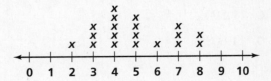

F 4

G 5

H 9

J 10

27. The stem-and-leaf plot below shows the weights of two dozen eggs.

Weight of Eggs (grams)

```
5 | 5 6 6 7 7 7 7 8 8 9 9 9
6 | 0 0 1 1 1 2 3 3 5 5 6
7 | 1
```

Key: 5|5 means 55 grams

What is the mode of the data?

A 55 grams

B 57 grams

C 60 grams

D 61 grams

28. John made a bar graph showing the eye colors of the sixth grade students at his school. How many more sixth grade students have brown eyes than blue eyes?

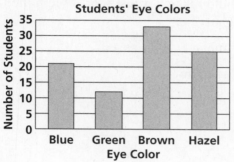

Students' Eye Colors

F   12

G   21

H   33

J   54

29. The graph below shows the favorite sports of students at a certain middle school. What sport is the most popular among girls at the school?

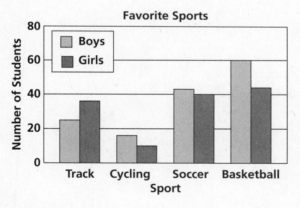

Favorite Sports

A   track

B   soccer

C   cycling

D   basketball

30. The line graph below shows the attendance at a museum over a period of five weeks. Which of the following statements is true?

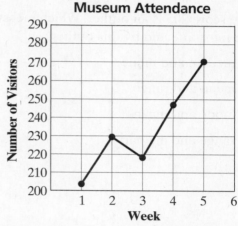

Museum Attendance

F   The museum was popular at first, but grew less so each week.

G   The museum attracted more visitors every week.

H   With one exception, the museum became more popular each week.

J   Attendance did not change over the weeks.

31. The graph below shows the amount of sales made by the employees of four bookstores. Which of the following best explains why the graph is misleading?

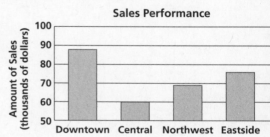

Sales Performance

A   The vertical scale does not begin at 0.

B   The bars are not arranged in order of height.

C   Each of the bars appears to have the same width.

D   The sales amounts are given in dollars instead of percents.

32. The list below shows a bowler's scores for her last five games.

205, 132, 140, 128, 132

The score 205 is an outlier. Which measures are most affected by this outlier?

F median and mode

G mean and range

H mode and mean

J range and median

33. Laura wants to convince her parents that she is doing well in science class. Her last five science test scores are 82, 99, 80, 80, and 79. Which measure of central tendency would make her test scores seem the highest?

A mean

B median

C mode

D range

Benchmark Test 2

1. Evaluate the expression $3.5x + 4$ for $x = 8$.

   A 28

   B 32

   C 60

   D 320

2. A taxi fare costs $3.00 plus $0.50 for each mile m. The expression $3 + 0.5m$ can be used to find any fare. What is the fare for a 13-mile taxi ride?

   F $3.50

   G $4.00

   H $7.00

   J $9.50

3. Evaluate the expression $3x - 2y$ for $x = 6$ and $y = 4$.

   A -8

   B 0

   C 6

   D 10

4. Which expression describes the relationship in the table below?

n	?
4	7
6.5	9.5
8	11

   F $n + 2$

   G $n + 2.5$

   H $n + 3$

   J $n + 3.5$

5. Glenn walks 3 kilometers per day. Which expression can be used to find the total number of kilometers Glenn has walked after d days?

   A $\dfrac{d}{3}$

   B $3d$

   C $3 + d$

   D $3d + 3$

6. On Wednesday mornings, admission to the park swimming pool is $3.00 per adult and $2.00 per child. Which expression can be used to find the cost of admission to the pool for a group of a adults and c children?

   F $3ac$

   G $5 + ac$

   H $3a + 2c$

   J $2(3) + a(c)$

7. Solve the following equation for k.

$$k - 72 = 118$$

A $k = 46$

B $k = 56$

C $k = 190$

D $k = 192$

8. What value for s makes the following equation true?

$$s + 4.28 = 7$$

F 2.72

G 4.21

H 11.28

J 28.28

9. Marta went to the craft store and spent $16.72 on supplies. She has $16.28 left to spend at the fabric store. Which equation can be used to find how much money, m, Marta had before she went to the craft store?

A $m - \$16.72 = \$16.28$

B $m + \$16.72 = \$16.28$

C $m = \$16.72 - \$16.28$

D $m + \$16.28 = \$16.72$

10. Solve the following equation for p.

$$p \times 4.8 = 16.8$$

F $p = 3.5$

G $p = 12$

H $p = 20$

J $p = 21.6$

11. What value of t makes the following equation true?

$$t \div 6 = 15.6$$

A 2.6

B 9.36

C 26

D 93.6

12. Jamie works in a discount card shop where every card is discounted by $0.75. If a customer saved $4.50, which equation can be used to determine the number of cards c the customer purchased?

F $0.75c = 4.50$

G $4.50c = 0.75$

H $c \div 0.75 = 4.50$

J $c \div 4.50 = 0.75$

13. Which of the following is equivalent to the expression $4(6 + 0.8)$?

A $(4 + 6) + (4 + 0.8)$

B $(4 + 6) \times (4 + 0.8)$

C $(4 \times 6) + (4 \times 0.8)$

D $(4 \times 6) \times (4 \times 0.8)$

14. Which of the following expressions is equivalent to 24×11?

F $(2 \times 11) + (4 \times 11)$

G $(20 \times 10) + (4 \times 1)$

H $(20 \times 11) + (4 \times 1)$

J $(24 \times 10) + (24 \times 1)$

15. Ms. Wilcox buys 3 plants that cost $1.95 each and 3 plants that cost $2.95 each. Which expression represents the total amount Ms. Wilcox spent?

A $3 \times \$4.90$

B $6 \times \$4.90$

C $3 \times (\$1.95 \times \$2.95)$

D $6 \times (\$1.95 \times \$2.95)$

16. Which of the following divisibility rules applies to divisibility by 6?

F The number must end in a 6.

G The number must be divisible by 2 only.

H The number must be divisible by 3 only.

J The number must be divisible by 2 and 3.

17. There are 12 adults and 30 students signed up for a field trip. Which could be the number of minivans needed to transport them if there are the same number of adults and the same number of students in each minivan?

A 4

B 5

C 6

D 12

18. Which digit will make the following number divisible by 9?

7,2■4

F 0

G 2

H 3

J 5

19. What is the value of the expression 4.2^3?

A 1.26

B 7.4088

C 12.6

D 74.088

20. Simplify the following expression.

$4^2 + 2^3$

F 14

G 24

H 1,056

J 7,776

21. Which exponent will make the following equation true?

$75 = 5^x \cdot 3$

A $x = 1$

B $x = 2$

C $x = 3$

D $x = 4$

22. Which of the following numbers is a prime number?

   F 111

   G 153

   H 227

   J 273

23. Which is the prime factorization of 120?

   A $2^3 \times 15$

   B $2^3 \times 3 \times 5$

   C $2 \times 3^3 \times 5$

   D $2 \times 3^2 \times 5^2$

24. Which of the following statements is *not* true about prime numbers?

   F No prime number is even.

   G Prime numbers are whole numbers.

   H Prime numbers have exactly two factors.

   J The numbers 0 and 1 are not prime numbers.

25. What is the greatest common factor (GCF) of 24 and 60?

   A 2

   B 3

   C 6

   D 12

26. Which of the following expressions describes the greatest common factor (GCF) of 72 and 108?

   F $2^2 \times 3^2$

   G $2^2 \times 3^3$

   H $2^3 \times 3^2$

   J $2^3 \times 3^3$

27. What is the greatest common factor of 60, 440, and 480?

   A 15

   B 20

   C 40

   D 60

28. Which of the following fractions is equivalent to $\frac{4}{9}$?

   F $\frac{2}{3}$

   G $\frac{8}{18}$

   H $\frac{8}{27}$

   J $\frac{16}{81}$

29. If the average person watches television for about three hours each day, for about what fraction of a full day does the average person watch TV?

   A $\frac{1}{8}$

   B $\frac{3}{7}$

   C $\frac{5}{12}$

   D $\frac{7}{24}$

30. A student flipped a coin 100 times, and the coin landed on heads 45 times. In simplest form, what fraction of the coin tosses landed on heads?

F $\frac{9}{20}$

G $\frac{1}{2}$

H $\frac{11}{20}$

J $\frac{4}{5}$

31. Which improper fraction is equivalent to the mixed number $6\frac{2}{3}$?

A $\frac{11}{3}$

B $\frac{12}{3}$

C $\frac{18}{3}$

D $\frac{20}{3}$

32. Each slice of pizza is $\frac{1}{6}$ of a whole pizza. How many pizzas are represented by 33 slices?

F $3\frac{1}{2}$ pizzas

G $4\frac{1}{2}$ pizzas

H $5\frac{1}{2}$ pizzas

J $6\frac{1}{2}$ pizzas

33. A recipe calls for $2\frac{1}{3}$ tablespoons of honey. How many teaspoons of honey does the recipe require? (Hint: 1 teaspoon = $\frac{1}{3}$ tablespoon.)

A 2 teaspoons

B 3 teaspoons

C 5 teaspoons

D 7 teaspoons

34. What is the least common multiple (LCM) of 12 and 15?

F 3

G 15

H 60

J 180

35. Often hot dogs are sold in packages of 12 and buns are sold in packages of 8. What is the *least* number of packages of hot dogs and buns that must be bought so that there is an equal number of each?

A 2 packages of hot dogs and 3 packages of buns

B 3 packages of hot dogs and 2 packages of buns

C 4 packages of hot dogs and 6 packages of buns

D 8 packages of hot dogs and 12 packages of buns

36. Pia runs every third day and swims every fourth day. How many days will it be before she performs both activities on the same day?

F   3 days

G   4 days

H   6 days

J   12 days

37. Where on the given number line is the fraction $\frac{5}{16}$ located?

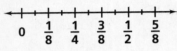

A   between $\frac{1}{8}$ and $\frac{1}{4}$

B   between $\frac{1}{4}$ and $\frac{3}{8}$

C   between $\frac{3}{8}$ and $\frac{1}{2}$

D   between $\frac{1}{2}$ and $\frac{5}{8}$

38. Which set of numbers is in order from least to greatest?

F $\frac{1}{4}, \frac{1}{5}, \frac{1}{6}$

G $\frac{1}{3}, \frac{5}{8}, \frac{4}{5}$

H $\frac{5}{6}, \frac{3}{4}, \frac{2}{3}$

J $\frac{3}{8}, \frac{2}{7}, \frac{1}{6}$

39. Which statement is *not* true?

A $0.1\overline{6} = \frac{1}{6}$

B $0.45 = \frac{9}{20}$

C $1.2 = 1\frac{2}{5}$

D $2.\overline{6} = \frac{8}{3}$

STOP

Benchmark Test 3

1. Estimate the difference.

$$4\frac{11}{20} - 1\frac{3}{8}$$

A 3

B $3\frac{1}{4}$

C $3\frac{1}{2}$

D 4

2. Which of the following is the *best* estimate for the sum $2\frac{5}{11} + 4\frac{7}{8}$?

F $6\frac{1}{2}$

G 7

H $7\frac{1}{2}$

J 8

3. Estimate to determine which of the following has the greatest value.

A the difference of $3\frac{1}{2}$ and $2\frac{1}{5}$

B the difference of $6\frac{2}{7}$ and $4\frac{1}{8}$

C the sum of $\frac{1}{2}$ and $\frac{1}{4}$

D the sum of $\frac{2}{5}$ and $\frac{1}{4}$

4. Find the difference.

$$\frac{7}{10} - \frac{1}{4}$$

F $\frac{9}{20}$

G $\frac{7}{25}$

H $\frac{9}{10}$

J 1

5. Terry shares a large muffin with her brother and sister. She gives $\frac{2}{7}$ of the muffin to her brother and $\frac{3}{8}$ to her sister. She keeps the rest for herself. Who received the largest piece of the muffin?

A Terry

B her brother

C her sister

D They all receive equal pieces.

6. On Monday, the water in a puddle had a height of $\frac{3}{16}$ inches. After a heavy rainfall on Tuesday, the height of the water in the puddle increased by $\frac{5}{8}$ of an inch. What is the total height of the water in the puddle after the rainfall?

F $\frac{7}{16}$ inches

G $\frac{13}{16}$ inches

H $\frac{13}{32}$ inches

J $\frac{8}{24}$ inches

7. Find the sum.

$$8\frac{2}{3} + 3\frac{4}{5}$$

A $11\frac{2}{5}$

B $11\frac{7}{15}$

C $11\frac{3}{4}$

D $12\frac{7}{15}$

8. Omar is riding his bike on the course at the park. After riding $14\frac{5}{8}$ miles he gets a flat tire. Omar walks the remaining $3\frac{2}{3}$ miles to complete the course. How long is the course?

F $17\frac{7}{11}$

G $17\frac{7}{24}$

H $17\frac{5}{12}$

J $18\frac{7}{24}$

9. Roz carves a stone sculpture weighing $5\frac{11}{25}$ kilograms. She then mounts the sculpture onto an acrylic base weighing $1\frac{7}{20}$ kilograms. What is the total weight of the mounted sculpture?

A $6\frac{79}{100}$ kilograms

B $6\frac{9}{50}$ kilograms

C $6\frac{18}{25}$ kilograms

D $6\frac{9}{10}$ kilograms

10. Find the difference.

$$3\frac{1}{3} - 2\frac{5}{6}$$

F $-\frac{1}{3}$

G $-\frac{1}{2}$

H $\frac{1}{2}$

J $1\frac{1}{2}$

11. Jane jumps rope for $6\frac{1}{2}$ minutes. Jesse jumps rope for $4\frac{3}{4}$ minutes. How many more minutes does Jane jump than Jesse?

A $1\frac{1}{2}$ minutes

B $1\frac{3}{4}$ minutes

C $2\frac{1}{4}$ minutes

D $2\frac{1}{2}$ minutes

12. It takes Max $2\frac{3}{4}$ hours to cut the grass using a push mower. If he uses the power mower, it takes $1\frac{1}{2}$ hours less time. How long does it take Max to cut the grass using the power mower?

F 1 hour

G $1\frac{1}{4}$ hours

H $1\frac{1}{2}$ hours

J $1\frac{3}{4}$ hours

13. What is the solution to the following equation?

$$\frac{3}{5} + x = 3\frac{7}{10}$$

A $1\frac{6}{25}$

B $1\frac{8}{25}$

C $3\frac{1}{10}$

D $3\frac{3}{5}$

14. Solve $\frac{5}{6} - \frac{1}{8} = n$.

F $-\frac{1}{2}$

G $\frac{1}{6}$

H $\frac{17}{24}$

J $\frac{3}{4}$

15. A spool contains $5\frac{1}{2}$ feet of ribbon. Pat cuts off a piece of ribbon. There are $3\frac{4}{5}$ feet of ribbon left on the spool. Which equation could *not* be used to determine the length of the ribbon (r) Pat cut off?

A $5\frac{1}{2} - r = 3\frac{4}{5}$

B $r + 3\frac{4}{5} = 5\frac{1}{2}$

C $5\frac{1}{2} - 3\frac{4}{5} = r$

D $r - 5\frac{1}{2} = 3\frac{4}{5}$

16. Find the product.

$$\frac{1}{3} \times \frac{1}{4}$$

F $\frac{1}{12}$

G $\frac{1}{6}$

H $\frac{7}{12}$

J $\frac{3}{4}$

17. A gardener weeded $\frac{3}{4}$ of a flower garden. If the garden has an area of 72 square yards, how many square yards did the gardener weed?

A 48 square yards

B 54 square yards

C 60 square yards

D 66 square yards

18. Three-fourths of the students in a gym class are girls. Two-thirds of the girls in the class play volleyball. What fraction of the gym students are girl volleyball players?

F $\frac{1}{4}$

G $\frac{1}{3}$

H $\frac{1}{2}$

J $\frac{5}{12}$

19. Which is the closest estimate of the product of $5\frac{1}{3}$ and $2\frac{3}{4}$?

A 8

B 10

C 15

D 18

20. Jorge's age is $1\frac{1}{2}$ times Jana's age. If Jana is 8 years old, how old is Jorge?

F $8\frac{1}{2}$

G $9\frac{1}{2}$

H 12

J 14

21. Last week, Lana worked $2\frac{1}{2}$ times as many hours as Shea. If Shea worked $15\frac{1}{3}$ hours, how many hours did Lana work?

A $30\frac{1}{3}$ hours

B $33\frac{2}{3}$ hours

C $38\frac{1}{3}$ hours

D $40\frac{1}{3}$ hours

22. Find the quotient.

$$\frac{2}{7} \div \frac{2}{3}$$

F $\frac{4}{21}$

G $\frac{1}{3}$

H $\frac{5}{14}$

J $\frac{3}{7}$

23. A spool contains 30 feet of ribbon. How many $\frac{3}{4}$-foot pieces of ribbon can be cut from the spool?

A 22

B 30

C 40

D 53

24. A restaurant's shrimp dinner includes $\frac{5}{8}$ pound of shrimp. How many shrimp dinners can the restaurant serve from a 20-pound bag of shrimp?

F 15

G 24

H 28

J 32

25. Find the quotient.

$$2\frac{1}{2} \div \frac{1}{4}$$

A $\frac{1}{10}$

B $\frac{5}{8}$

C 8

D 10

26. A pancake recipe calls for $\frac{3}{4}$ of a cup of milk for each batch. How many batches of pancakes can Alex make with $3\frac{3}{4}$ cups of milk?

F 4

G $4\frac{3}{4}$

H 5

J $5\frac{1}{2}$

27. An airport shuttle van charges $0.25 for every $\frac{1}{5}$ of a mile. If a trip to the airport is $3\frac{6}{10}$ miles, how much does the shuttle service cost?

A $4.50

B $4.75

C $5.00

D $5.25

28. What is the value of d in the following equation?

$$\frac{5}{6}d = 15$$

F 18

G 24

H 30

J 36

29. The cost of a package of computer paper is $\frac{1}{8}$ the cost of a cartridge of printer ink. The price of an ink cartridge is $28.95. Which equation can be used to find the cost of a package of computer paper, p?

A $p = \frac{1}{8} \cdot 28.95$

B $\frac{8}{p} = 28.95$

C $\frac{1}{8}p = 28.95$

D $p = 8 \cdot 28.95$

30. Which of the following equations does *not* have a solution of $x = 8$?

F $2x = 16$

G $\frac{1}{4}x = 2$

H $\frac{x}{4} = 32$

J $\frac{24}{x} = 3$

31. Lacy has 18 bricks that are each 8 inches long. If she lays the bricks end to end to make a path, what will be the length of the path in feet?

A 12 feet

B 15 feet

C 18 feet

D 21 feet

32. The length of the longest runway at the Orlando Sanford International Airport is 9,600 feet. To the nearest tenth of a mile, how many miles long is this runway?

F 1.6 miles

G 1.7 miles

H 1.8 miles

J 1.9 miles

33. June bought 5 gallons of punch for the spring dance. How many cups of punch did she buy?

A   32 cups

B 80 cups

C 160 cups

D 640 cups

Benchmark Test 4

1. During an 8-hour shift, a highway toll collector collected 672 tolls. What was the hourly toll collection rate?

   A 81 tolls per hour

   B 82 tolls per hour

   C 83 tolls per hour

   D 84 tolls per hour

2. It took Trina 1 hour and 15 minutes to shovel the snow from her neighbor's driveway. During that time she burned 525 Calories. How many Calories per minute did Trina burn while shoveling snow?

   F 5 Calories per minute

   G 7 Calories per minute

   H 8 Calories per minute

   J 9 Calories per minute

3. Ian's favorite brand of frozen waffles is sold in 4 different sizes. Which size box is the best buy (lowest cost per waffle)?

   Frozen Waffles

Size of Box	Number of Waffles	Cost per Box
Regular	8	$1.28
Large	12	$1.80
Extra large	16	$2.08
Jumbo	24	$3.36

   A regular

   B large

   C extra large

   D jumbo

4. Which pair of ratios does *not* form a proportion?

   F $\frac{5}{8}$ and $\frac{15}{24}$

   G $\frac{7}{9}$ and $\frac{9}{7}$

   H $\frac{3}{8}$ and $\frac{15}{40}$

   J $\frac{15}{18}$ and $\frac{105}{126}$

5. A local grocery store is advertising a special on picnic supplies. Charcoal is priced at 3 bags for $11.50. Use the following proportion to find the cost of 5 bags of charcoal.

   $$\frac{3}{11.50} = \frac{5}{x}$$

   A $15.50

   B $18.40

   C $19.17

   D $22.75

6. What is the value of f in the proportion shown below?

   $$\frac{10 \text{ meters}}{32.8 \text{ feet}} = \frac{25 \text{ meters}}{f}$$

   F 80 feet

   G 81 feet

   H 82 feet

   J 83 feet

7. A long-distance runner ran 15 miles in 105 minutes. If her rate is constant, how many minutes does it take her to run 1 mile?

   A 6 minutes   **C** 8 minutes

   B 7 minutes   **D** 9 minutes

8. An 8-ounce serving of soup contains 19 grams of carbohydrates. To the nearest gram, how many grams of carbohydrates does a 5-ounce serving of soup contain?

   F 10 grams   H 12 grams

   G 11 grams   J 13 grams

9. If 7 AA batteries cost $3.29, how much will 12 AA batteries cost?

   A $5.64   C $5.82

   B $5.66   D $5.88

10. Marcus builds model cars. Listed below are the actual lengths of each car and the lengths of each of his models. If the scale for each car is the same, what scale does Marcus use?

   Marcus's Models

Model Car	Actual Length	Model Length
sports car	12 feet	6 inches
compact car	8 feet	4 inches
light truck	15 feet	7.5 inches

   F 1 inch = $\frac{1}{2}$ foot

   G 1 inch = 1 foot

   H 1 inch = $1\frac{1}{2}$ feet

   J 1 inch = 2 feet

11. The distance on a map from Centerville to Louisburg is $2\frac{1}{2}$ inches. The scale on the map is 1 inch = 50 miles. What is the actual distance between Centerville and Louisburg?

   A 100 miles   C 150 miles

   B 125 miles   D 175 miles

12. The Eiffel Tower in France is approximately 300 meters tall. Jeremy is making a model of this famous landmark. His scale is 0.5 cm = 3 meters. How tall should his model be?

   F 30 cm   H 50 cm

   G 45 cm   J 60 cm

13. What is 42% of 550?

   A 76   C 231

   B 131   D 508

14. The rugby team won 10 games and lost 6 games. What percent of their games did the rugby team win?

   F 60.4%   H 65.5%

   G 62.5%   J 66.7%

15. Eighteen of 50 students went to the beach for an extra credit science project. What percent of the students did *not* go to the beach?

   A 18%   C 64%

   B 32%   D 82%

16. Twenty-four students were surveyed about their favorite type of shoes. Fourteen chose sneakers, 6 chose sandals, and 4 chose boots. Jacob plans to make a circle graph of the survey results. What percent of the circle graph should represent students who chose sandals?

   F 14%   H 40%

   G 25%   J 60%

17. Margo asked 50 students at her school how many pets they owned. The circle graph below shows the results of Margo's survey.

Pet Survey

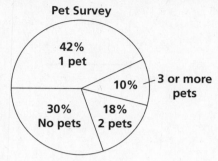

42%
1 pet

10% 3 or more pets

30% No pets

18% 2 pets

What percent of the students surveyed own 2 pets?

A 10%   **C** 30%

B 18%   **D** 42%

18. In which scenario is a circle graph most appropriate?

F the change in gasoline prices over time

G how many students within a school prefer certain kinds of sports

H the populations of several different cities

J a positive trend in students' grades over the years

19. Luke's dinner bill is $35.89. He plans to leave a 20% tip. Which of the following is the closest estimate of the tip?

A $7.00   **C** $9.00

B $8.00   **D** $10.00

20. The estimated cost to repair Chen's bicycle is $29.95. The owner of the bike shop tells Chen that the actual cost to repair the bike will be no higher than 10% more than the estimated cost. Which is the closest estimate of the most Chen can expect to pay for the bicycle repair?

F $30.00   **H** $32.00

G $31.00   **J** $33.00

21. Sue's bank pays her a simple yearly interest rate of 4.8% on the money in her college savings account. She opens her account with $812. Which is the closest estimate of the amount of interest her account will have earned after one year?

A $30

B $32

C $40

D $42

22. The diagram below shows a portion of a map. Which pair of streets are parallel?

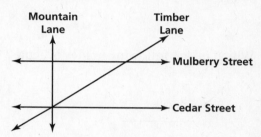

Mountain Lane   Timber Lane

Mulberry Street

Cedar Street

F Cedar Street and Timber Lane

G Mountain Lane and Mulberry Street

H Timber Lane and Mountain Lane

J Mulberry Street and Cedar Street

23. Which of the following is a characteristic of intersecting lines?

A They are skew to one another.

B They are parallel to one another.

C They have no points in common.

D They have a single point in common.

24. Which segment in the figure below is parallel to $\overline{EF}$ and skew to $\overline{AD}$?

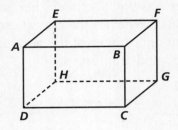

F $\overline{AB}$

G $\overline{AE}$

H $\overline{CD}$

J $\overline{GH}$

25. Which of the following angles is acute?

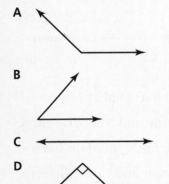

A

B

C

D

26. At which of the following times do the minute and hour hands of a clock form a straight angle?

F 1:00

G 3:00

H 6:00

J 10:00

27. Which is the closest estimate of the measure of $\angle DEF$?

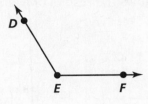

A 60°

B 90°

C 120°

D 180°

28. Which term best describes angles 3 and 6 in the figure below?

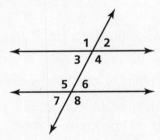

F exterior angles

G interior angles

H obtuse angles

J vertical angles

29. What is the measure of $\angle RST$ in the figure below?

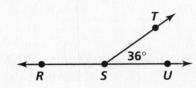

A 54°

B 64°

C 136°

D 144°

Name _____ Class _____ Date _____

30. What is the value of *x* in the figure below?

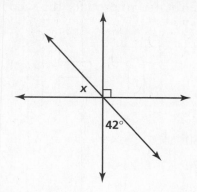

F 42° H 132°

G 48° J 138°

31. What type of triangle is shown below?

A equilateral triangle

B obtuse triangle

C right triangle

D scalene triangle

32. What two shapes are created when a square is divided by one diagonal?

F two acute isosceles triangles

G two obtuse scalene triangles

H two right isosceles triangles

J two right scalene triangles

33. Two angles of a triangular sail measure 65° and 40°. What is the measure of the third angle of the sail?

A 15°

B 25°

C 75°

D 105°

34. What type of polygon is shown below?

F hexagon H pentagon

G octagon J quadrilateral

35. Which of the following quadrilaterals is *not* a parallelogram?

A square C rhombus

B rectangle D trapezoid

36. How is a rhombus different from a square?

F Unlike a rhombus, a square must have 4 right angles.

G Unlike a rhombus, a square must have 4 congruent sides.

H Unlike a square, a rhombus must have 4 congruent angles.

J Unlike a square, a rhombus must have 2 pairs of parallel sides.

37. Which of the following pairs of pentagons appear to be congruent?

A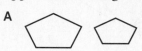

B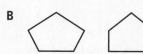

C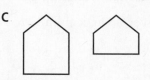

D

Benchmark Test 4 *Course 1* **29**

38. The trapezoids shown below are congruent. Which angle is congruent to ∠*NML*?

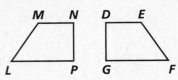

F ∠*DEF*

G ∠*EFG*

H ∠*FGD*

J ∠*GDE*

39. If the triangles shown below are congruent, what is the value of *x*?

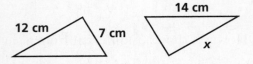

A 7 centimeters

B 12 centimeters

C 14 centimeters

D 24 centimeters

40. Which of the following best describes the transformation shown below?

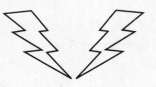

F a rotation of 90°

G a rotation of 180°

H a reflection over a horizontal line

J a reflection over a vertical line

41. How many degrees clockwise was the first figure rotated to produce the second figure?

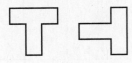

A 90°

B 180°

C 270°

D 360°

42. Which figure represents a translation of the figure shown below?

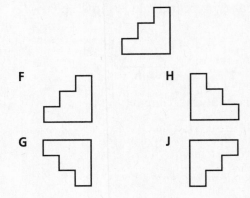

F

H

G

J

STOP

Benchmark Test 5

1. Which is the most appropriate unit of measurement to use to find the mass of a pencil?

   A gram

   B meter

   C kilogram

   D centimeter

2. What is the mass, in grams, of a brick that has a mass of 5.5 kilograms?

   F 0.0055 gram

   G 0.055 gram

   H 550 grams

   J 5,500 grams

3. The height of a fence is 125 centimeters. What is the height of the fence in meters?

   A 0.125 meter

   B 1.25 meters

   C 12.5 meters

   D 1,250 meters

4. A lake is shown on the grid below. Each square represents 6 square miles. Which is the best estimate of the area of the lake?

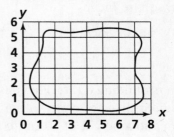

   F 120 square miles

   G 180 square miles

   H 240 square miles

   J 300 square miles

5. A rectangular garden has a length of 8 meters and a width of 6 meters. What is the area of the garden?

   A 14 square meters

   B 28 square meters

   C 48 square meters

   D 64 square meters

6. What is the area of a square that has a perimeter of 32 feet?

   F 8 square feet

   G 16 square feet

   H 32 square feet

   J 64 square feet

7. What is the area of a parallelogram with a height of 9 inches and a base length of 12 inches?

   A 44 square inches

   B 54 square inches

   C 88 square inches

   D 108 square inches

8. Ryan is building a kite. He is using a triangular piece of cloth with a base of 50 cm and a height of 30 cm to cover the frame. What is the area of the piece of cloth?

   F 80 square centimeters

   G 160 square centimeters

   H 750 square centimeters

   J 1,500 square centimeters

9. What is the area of the figure below?

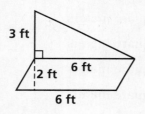

   A 15 square feet

   B 21 square feet

   C 24 square feet

   D 36 square feet

10. A circular window has a diameter of 40 centimeters. What is the circumference of the window? Use 3.14 for π.

   F 62.8 cm

   G 125.6 cm

   H 251.2 cm

   J 502.4 cm

11. What is the radius of a circle that has a circumference of 7.85 meters? Use 3.14 for π.

   A 1.25 m

   B 2.5 m

   C 24.65 m

   D 42.3 m

12. What is the area, to the nearest tenth, of the circular rug shown below? Use 3.14 for π.

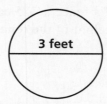

   F 4.7 square feet

   G 7.1 square feet

   H 9.4 square feet

   J 18.8 square feet

13. How many faces does a cube have?

    A 4

    B 6

    C 8

    D 9

14. What is the name of the figure shown below?

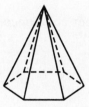

    F triangular prism

    G hexagonal prism

    H triangular pyramid

    J hexagonal pyramid

15. How many vertices does the figure shown below have?

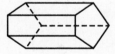

    A 5

    B 7

    C 10

    D 15

16. What is the surface area of the cylinder shown below? Use 3.14 for π.

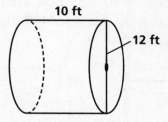

10 ft

12 ft

    F 188.4 square feet

    G 376.8 square feet

    H 602.9 square feet

    J 1,130.4 square feet

17. A cereal box that is shaped like a rectangular prism has a length of 8 inches, a width of 3 inches, and a height of 12 inches. What is the volume of the cereal box?

    A 144 cubic inches

    B 156 cubic inches

    C 288 cubic inches

    D 312 cubic inches

18. At a hardware store, paint is sold in two different sizes of cans. The dimensions of each can are shown below. What is the volume of the can that holds the *most* paint? Use 3.14 for π.

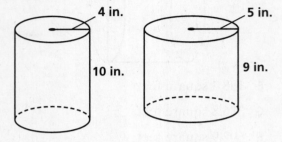

4 in.   5 in.

10 in.   9 in.

F 502.4 cubic inches

G 706.5 cubic inches

H 1,413.1 cubic inches

J 2,009.6 cubic inches

19. A café has 3 entrees, 5 sides, and 4 desserts. If you choose one item from each category, how many different meals can you order?

A 60

B 30

C 20

D 15

20. A mother wants to arrange her 4 children for a photograph. In how many ways can she line her children up, side-by-side, from left to right?

F 4

G 12

H 24

J 120

21. School has just begun. You have four shirts, three pairs of pants, and two pairs of shoes. How many days can you make it without wearing the same outfit twice?

A 3

B 4

C 12

D 24

22. You roll a number cube once. Find $P(6)$.

F $\frac{1}{2}$

G $\frac{1}{3}$

H $\frac{1}{4}$

J $\frac{1}{6}$

23. Of 18 students in a class, 10 are girls. The teacher selects a student at random. What is $P(\text{not a girl})$?

A $\frac{2}{3}$

B $\frac{5}{9}$

C $\frac{4}{9}$

D $\frac{1}{3}$

24. A bag contains 5 red marbles, 3 green marbles, and 4 yellow marbles. You select a marble at random. Find $P(\text{green})$.

F $\frac{1}{2}$

G $\frac{1}{3}$

H $\frac{1}{4}$

J $\frac{1}{6}$

25. You flip a coin 8 times. Five of those times it lands on heads. What is the experimental probability that the coin lands on heads?

A 5%

B 50%

C 37.5%

D 62.5%

26. A basketball player makes 9 out of 15 free throws. Find the experimental probability of the player making a free throw.

F $\frac{1}{2}$

G $\frac{2}{3}$

H $\frac{3}{4}$

J $\frac{3}{5}$

27. Out of the five times he went to school this week, Peter missed the bus 2 times. What is the experimental probability that Peter misses the bus?

A 25 %

B 40 %

C 50 %

D 60 %

28. A company makes 20,000 motors. The company inspects a random sample of 250 motors. The sample has 15 faulty motors. Predict how many of the 20,000 motors are likely to be faulty.

F 50

G 600

H 1,200

J 5,000

29. In a school survey, 65 out of 75 students said they participate in extracurricular sports activities. The school has 500 students. Predict the number of students who participate in extracurricular sports activities.

A 388

B 417

C 433

D 452

30. Out of a shipment of 50 bicycle inner tubes, 3 are defective. How many defective inner tubes will there probably be in a shipment of 400 inner tubes?

F 3

G 12

H 24

J 50

31. Which events are not independent events?

  A You select a card from a deck of cards. Without replacing it, you select another card.

  B You select a marble from a bag. You return the marble to the bag and draw another one.

  C You spin a spinner twice. The pointer stops in two different places.

  D You roll three number cubes, and the numbers rolled are 5, 6, and 2.

32. Twenty cards are numbered 1–20. You draw a card, return it to the deck, and then draw a second card. Find P(even, then odd).

  F $\frac{1}{2}$

  G $\frac{1}{3}$

  H $\frac{1}{4}$

  J $\frac{1}{5}$

33. You guess the answers on two multiple choice questions (choices A, B, C, D) and two true-or-false questions. What is the probability that all four answers are correct?

  A $\frac{1}{64}$

  B $\frac{1}{16}$

  C $\frac{1}{12}$

  D $\frac{1}{3}$

34. Which of the following is the opposite of the number graphed on the number line below?

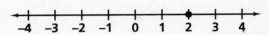

  F -4

  G -2

  H 0

  J 2

35. Which list shows the numbers 8, -5, -12, and -2 in order from least to greatest?

  A $-12, -5, -2, 8$

  B $-2, -5, -12, 8$

  C $-12, -5, 8, -2$

  D $-2, -5, 8, -12$

36. Which comparison is *not* true?

  F $|-6| > |5|$

  G $-8 < -7$

  H $|14| < |-15|$

  J $-12 > -11$

37. What is $(-8) + 11 + (-5)$?

  A -24

  B -2

  C 3

  D 14

38. Which expression has a sum of −13?

   F 8 + 5

   G −11 + 2

   H 6 + (−7)

   J −4 + (−9)

39. What is the value of −15−(−33)?

   A −48

   B −18

   C 18

   D 48

40. The temperature dropped 3°F each hour over an 8-hour period. Which integer represents the total change in temperature?

   F −24°F

   G −11°F

   H 24°F

   J 11°F

41. The elevation of the South Kaibib Trail in Grand Canyon National Park decreases 1,480 feet over 2 miles. What is the average rate of change in feet per mile?

   A −2,960 feet per mile

   B −740 feet per mile

   C 740 feet per mile

   D 2,960 feet per mile

42. Solve for m.

$$-7m = -42$$

   F −49

   G −6

   H 6

   J 49

43. What is the missing value in the function table below?

Input	Output
4	1
6	3
8	5
10	7
12	?

   A 3

   B 6

   C 9

   D 11

44. The science club is ordering T-shirts by mail. The shirts cost $12 each and there is a $4 shipping charge. The function $C = 4 + 12s$ shows the total cost C of ordering s T-shirts. What will be the total cost of 10 T-shirts?

   F $120

   G $124

   H $160

   J $164

45. Which graph shows the function
$y = -3x + 2$?

A

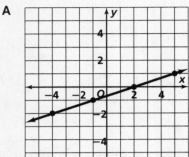

B

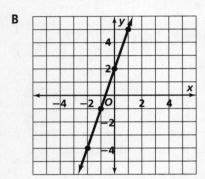

C

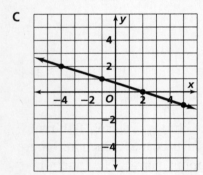

D

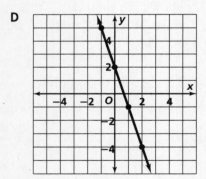

STOP

Quarter 1 Test

Chapters 1–3

Form A

1. Write the decimal that the model represents. Then write a decimal for the portion of the model that is not shaded.

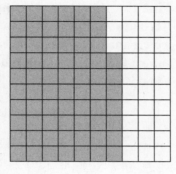

2. Write 11.017 in words.

3. Write the number in standard form.
   200,000 + 6,000 + 90 + 6 + 0.04

4. Use <, >, or = to complete the statement.
   0.35 __?__ 0.4

5. Round 19.082 to the nearest tenth.

6. Use compatible numbers to estimate.
   47.9 ÷ 5.99

7. Allen had $312.18 in his checking account. He wrote a check for $37.12. Find his new balance.

8. Use the data in the chart below. Suppose you have to limit your sugar intake to 2 oz per day.

Food	Sugar Content
Orange juice (4 oz)	0.417 oz
Plain granola bar	0.333 oz
Raisins (7 oz)	0.75 oz
Yogurt (8 oz)	1 oz

   a. How many ounces of sugar did you consume if you drank 8 oz of orange juice and ate two granola bars?

   b. Did you go over your daily limit?

9. Place the decimal point in the product. Write zeros as necessary.

   $$\begin{array}{r} 1.03 \\ \times\ 0.04 \\ \hline 412 \end{array}$$

10. At $1.75 per pound, what will 2.25 pounds of grapes cost?

11. Divide. 644.8 ÷ 0.8

12. Use mental math to find the product.
    123.62 × 1,000

13. Evaluate. 8 × (45 ÷ 4.5) + 20

14. Write the next two terms in the pattern.
    1, 3.5, 6, 8.5, …

15. Evaluate the expression.
    $6p - 11$ for $p = 5$

16. In the expression $m - 5$, replace m with $4m + 10$. Simplify the resulting expression.

17. Write an algebraic expression for the word phrase "p decreased by 9."

18. Tell whether the given number is a solution to the equation.
    $7x - 5 = 16$; 3

19. Explain what you would do to each side of the equation to solve it.
    $x - 17 = 30$

20. Tom weighs 42 pounds more than his sister. If Tom weighs 90 pounds, how much does his sister weigh?

21. You have three times as many baseball cards as your friend. Your friend has 150 cards. Write an expression that represents the number of cards you have.

22. Solve the equation.
$1.2b = 3.6$

23. Write 23,400,000 in scientific notation.

24. $3 \times 17 = (3 \times 10) + (3 \times 7)$ is an example of what property?

25. Evaluate the expression $6(x - 4)$, if $x = 5.5$.

Use the data below for Exercises 26 and 27.

45, 36, 34, 41, 55, 44, 46, 41, 38

26. What is the mean of this data?

27. What is the range of this data?

Andre surveyed the students in his class to find the number of books each student read last month. Use the line plot below for Exercises 28 and 29.

Number of Books Read Last Month

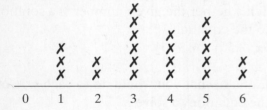

28. How many students read at least three books?

29. How many students read books last month?

Mrs. Van Zandt's class conducted a survey of Grisham Middle School to find what flavor of ice cream the students liked best. The results are shown in the bar graph below. Use the graph for Exercises 30–32.

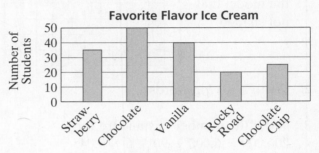

30. How many students liked chocolate chip ice cream the best?

31. How many more students liked chocolate ice cream than strawberry?

32. Which flavor did the greatest number of students like best?

A.J. made a stem-and-leaf plot of his quiz scores in math class this month. Use A.J.'s table below for Exercises 33–35.

Math Test Scores

8	0 1 1 3 4 7 8
9	0 2 5 5 5 9
10	0 0

Key: 8 | 0 means 80

33. What was A.J.'s mean score?

34. What was A.J.'s median score?

35. What is the range of A.J.'s quiz scores?

Quarter 1 Test

Chapters 1–3

Form B

1. Write the decimal that the model represents. Then write a decimal for the portion of the model that is not shaded.

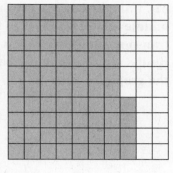

2. Write 319.05 in words.

3. Write the number in standard form.
$90,000 + 800 + 40 + 0.1 + 0.003$

4. Use $<$, $>$, or $=$ to complete the statement.
1.5 __?__ 1.05

5. Round 11.437 to the nearest hundredth.

6. Use compatible numbers to estimate.
39×6.97

7. Martha had $1,042.86 in her savings account. She deposited $128.25. Find her new balance.

8. Use the data in the chart below. Suppose you have to limit your sugar intake to 2 oz per day.

Food	Sugar Content
Orange juice (4 oz)	0.417 oz
Plain granola bar	0.333 oz
Raisins (7 oz)	0.75 oz
Yogurt (8 oz)	1 oz

   a. How many ounces of sugar did you consume if you drank 12 oz of orange juice and ate 8 oz of yogurt?

   b. Did you go over your daily limit?

9. Place the decimal point in the product. Write zeros as necessary.

$$\begin{array}{r} 3.4 \\ \times\ 0.02 \\ \hline 68 \end{array}$$

10. At $1.45 per pound, what will 2.5 pounds of grapes cost?

11. Divide. $0.765 \div 1.5$

12. Use mental math to find the quotient.
$85.2 \div 1,000$

13. Evaluate. $36 \div (1.2 \times 10) + 20$

14. Write the next two terms in the pattern.
$0.75, 2, 3.25, 4.5, \ldots$

15. Evaluate the expression.
$9t + 6$ for $t = 4$

16. In the expression $k + 11$, replace k with $6k - 1$. Simplify the resulting expression.

17. Write an algebraic expression for the word phrase "y increased by 4."

18. Tell whether the given number is a solution to the equation.
$15x + 2 = 50; 3$

19. Explain what you would do to each side of the equation to solve it.
$y + 15 = 40$

20. David's sister weighs 22 pounds less than he does. If his sister weighs 65 pounds, how much does David weigh?

Quarter 1 Test (continued)

Chapters 1–3

Form B

21. You have 20 more baseball cards than your friend does. Write an expression that represents the number of cards you have.

22. Solve the equation.
$d \div 9 = 7$

23. Write 0.000619 in scientific notation.

24. $9(w - 12) = (9 \times w) - (9 \times 12)$ is an example of what property?

25. Evaluate the expression $8(2 + x)$, if $x = 0.5$.

Use the data below for Exercises 26 and 27.

42, 16, 8, 15, 4, 23, 108

26. What is the mean of this data?

27. What is the range of this data?

Dennis surveys the students in his class to find the number of hours each student spent doing homework the previous week. Use the line plot below for Exercises 28 and 29.

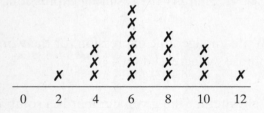

Hours Spent on Homework

28. How many students spent 4 hours on homework?

29. How many hours did the greatest number of students spend on homework?

Mr. Campbell's class conducted a survey of middle school teachers to find what type of transportation they use to get to school. The results are shown in the bar graph below. Use the graph for Exercises 30–32.

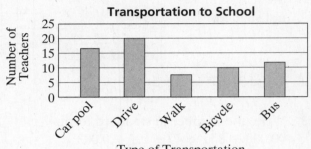

30. How many teachers ride the bus to work?

31. How many more teachers drive to work than ride bicycles?

32. Do more teachers walk or participate in a car pool?

Tito made a stem-and-leaf plot of the points he scored in several basketball games. Use Tito's table below for Exercises 33–35.

Basketball Scores

```
1 | 0 2 4 5 5 8 9
2 | 0 1 1 2 3 3
3 | 0 2
```
Key: 1 | 0 means 10

33. What was Tito's mean score?

34. What was Tito's median score?

35. What is the range of Tito's basketball scores?

Quarter 1 Test

Form D

Chapters 1–3

1. Write the decimal that the model represents. Then write a decimal for the portion of the model that is not shaded.

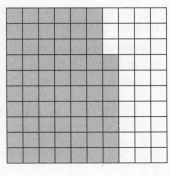

2. Write 11.017 in words.

3. Write the number in standard form.
$200,000 + 6,000 + 90 + 6 + 0.04$

4. Use $<$, $>$, or $=$ to complete the statement.
$0.35 \underline{\ ?\ } 0.4$

5. Round 19.082 to the nearest tenth.

6. Use compatible numbers to estimate.
$47.9 \div 5.99$

7. Allen had $312.18 in his checking account. He wrote a check for $37.12. Find his new balance.

8. Use the data in the chart below. Suppose you have to limit your sugar intake to 2 oz per day.

Food	Sugar Content
Orange juice (4 oz)	0.417 oz
Plain granola bar	0.333 oz
Raisins (7 oz)	0.75 oz
Yogurt (8 oz)	1 oz

a. How many ounces of sugar did you consume if you drank 8 oz of orange juice and ate two granola bars?

b. Did you go over your daily limit?

9. Evaluate. $8 \times (45 \div 4.5) + 20$

10. Write the next two terms in the pattern.
$1, 3.5, 6, 8.5, \ldots$

11. Evaluate the expression.
$6p - 11$ for $p = 5$

12. In the expression $m - 5$, replace m with $4m + 10$. Write the resulting solution.

13. Write an algebraic expression for the word phrase "p decreased by 9."

14. Explain what you would do to each side of the equation to solve it.
$x - 17 = 30$

15. Tom weighs 42 pounds more than his sister. If Tom weighs 90 pounds, how much does his sister weigh?

16. You have three times as many baseball cards as your friend. Your friend has 150 cards. Write an expression that represents the number of cards you have.

17. Solve the equation.
$1.2b = 3.6$

18. Write 23,400,000 in scientific notation.

19. $3 \times 17 = (3 \times 10) + (3 \times 7)$ is an example of what property?

20. Evaluate the expression $6(x - 4)$, if $x = 5.5$.

Use the data below for Exercises 21 and 22.

$$45, 36, 34, 41, 55, 44, 46, 41, 38$$

21. What is the mean of this data?

22. What is the range of this data?

Andre surveyed the students in his class to find the number of books each student read last month. Use the line plot below for Exercises 23 and 24.

Number of Books Read Last Month

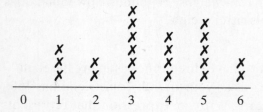

23. How many students read at least three books?

24. How many students read books last month?

Mrs. Van Zandt's class conducted a survey of Grisham Middle School to find what flavor of ice cream the students liked best. The results are shown in the bar graph below. Use the graph for Exercises 25 and 26.

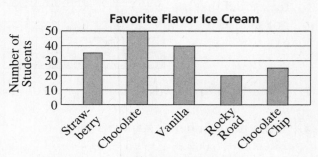

25. How many students liked chocolate chip ice cream the best?

26. Which flavor did the greatest number of students like best?

A.J. made a stem-and-leaf plot of his quiz scores in math class this month. Use A.J.'s table below for Exercises 27 and 28.

Math Test Scores

```
 8 | 0 1 1 3 4 7 8
 9 | 0 2 5 5 5 9
10 | 0 0
```
Key: 8 | 0 means 80

27. What was A.J.'s mean score?

28. What is the range of A.J.'s quiz scores?

Quarter 1 Test

Form E

Chapters 1–3

1. Write the decimal that the model represents. Then write a decimal for the portion of the model that is not shaded.

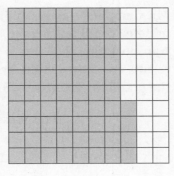

2. Write 319.05 in words.

3. Write the number in standard form.
   $90,000 + 800 + 40 + 0.1 + 0.003$

4. Use $<$, $>$, or $=$ to complete the statement.
   1.5 __?__ 1.05

5. Round 11.437 to the nearest hundredth.

6. Use compatible numbers to estimate.
   39×6.97

7. Martha had $1,042.86 in her savings account. She deposited $128.25. Find her new balance.

8. Use the data in the chart below. Suppose you have to limit your sugar intake to 2 oz per day.

Food	Sugar Content
Orange juice (4 oz)	0.417 oz
Plain granola bar	0.333 oz
Raisins (7 oz)	0.75 oz
Yogurt (8 oz)	1 oz

   a. How many ounces of sugar did you consume if you drank 12 oz of orange juice and ate 8 oz of yogurt?

   b. Did you go over your daily limit?

9. Evaluate. $36 \div (1.2 \times 10) + 20$

10. Write the next two terms in the pattern.
    0.75, 2, 3.25, 4.5, . . .

11. Evaluate the expression.
    $9t + 6$ for $t = 4$

12. In the expression $k + 11$, replace k with $6k - 1$. Write the resulting solution.

13. Write an algebraic expression for the word phrase "y increased by 4."

14. Explain what you would do to each side of the equation to solve it.
    $y + 15 = 40$

15. David's sister weighs 22 pounds less than he does. If his sister weighs 65 pounds, how much does David weigh?

16. You have 20 more baseball cards than your friend does. Write an expression that represents the number of cards you have.

17. Solve the equation.
    $d \div 9 = 7$

18. Write 0.000619 in scientific notation.

Chapters 1–3

19. $9(w - 12) = (9 \times w) - (9 \times 12)$ is an example of what property?

20. Evaluate the expression $8(2 + x)$, if $x = 0.5$.

Use the data below for Exercises 21 and 22.

42, 16, 8, 15, 4, 23, 108

21. What is the mean of this data?

22. What is the range of this data?

Dennis surveys the students in his class to find the number of hours each student spent doing homework the previous week. Use the line plot below for Exercises 23 and 24.

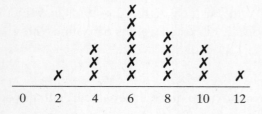

Hours Spent on Homework

23. How many students spent 4 hours on homework?

24. How many hours did most students spend on homework?

Mr. Campbell's class conducted a survey of middle school teachers to find what type of transportation they use to get to school. The results are shown in the bar graph below. Use the graph for Exercises 25 and 26.

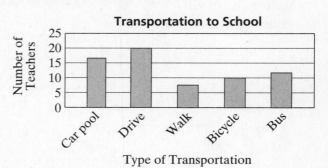

25. How many teachers ride the bus to work?

26. Do more teachers walk or participate in a car pool?

Tito made a stem-and-leaf plot of the points he scored in several basketball games. Use Tito's table below for Exercises 27 and 28.

Basketball Scores

```
1 | 0 2 4 5 5 8 9
2 | 0 1 1 2 3 3
3 | 0 2
```
Key: 1 | 0 means 10

27. What was Tito's mean score?

28. What is the range of Tito's basketball scores?

Quarter 2 Test   Form A
Chapters 4–6

1. Use mental math to determine whether 22,645 is divisible by 9.

2. Use a factor tree to find the prime factorization of 120. Write your answer using exponents.

3. Find the GCF of 24, 72, and 96.

4. If you were to plot the fractions $\frac{3}{12}$ and $\frac{1}{4}$ on the same number line, where would they be in relation to each other?

5. Write a fraction with a denominator of 18 that is equivalent to $\frac{2}{3}$.

6. Write $\frac{44}{6}$ as a mixed number.

7. Find the LCM of 18 and 30.

8. Order the mixed numbers from least to greatest.
   $3\frac{4}{7}, 3\frac{8}{15}, 3\frac{1}{2}$

9. Fill in the __?__ with $<$, $>$, or $=$.
   $\frac{23}{9}$ __?__ $2\frac{10}{18}$

10. Write 0.135 as a fraction in simplest form.

11. Write $6\frac{7}{20}$ as a decimal.

12. Write six and two fifths as a decimal.

13. The sum of two decimals is 1.2. One of the decimals is twice the other. What are the two decimals?

14. Round $11\frac{7}{12}$ to the nearest whole number.

15. Estimate $7\frac{4}{5} + 9\frac{1}{12}$ by first rounding to the nearest whole number.

16. Add. Write your answer in simplest form.
    $\frac{3}{20} + \frac{7}{20} - \frac{2}{20}$

17. Explain how you would add the fractions $\frac{1}{2}$ and $\frac{3}{4}$.

18. Sean rode his bicycle $4\frac{1}{4}$ miles on Saturday and $5\frac{7}{8}$ miles on Sunday. How many miles did he ride during the weekend?

19. Add. Write your answer in simplest form.
    $11\frac{1}{2} + 3\frac{4}{5} + 6\frac{1}{3}$

20. There are two boards leaning against the wall. The first board is $3\frac{5}{8}$ meters long and the second is $4\frac{1}{4}$ meters long. How much longer is the second board?

21. What is the first step in solving the equation $x + 1\frac{5}{6} = 5$?

22. Solve the equation. Write your answer in simplest form.
$$x - 3\frac{11}{12} = 6\frac{5}{12}$$

23. Find the elapsed time from 8:35 A.M. to 10:15 A.M.

24. Which product is NOT equal to the others?

    A. $\frac{1}{2} \cdot \frac{8}{5}$ B. $\frac{5}{4} \cdot \frac{16}{25}$ C. $\frac{5}{2} \cdot \frac{1}{2}$ D. $\frac{1}{5} \cdot \frac{4}{1}$

25. A chocolate pie has a total of about 2,200 calories. The pie is divided into 8 equal slices. Write an expression using a fraction to calculate the number of calories in each slice. Then calculate the number of calories in each slice.

26. Find the product. Write your answer as a mixed number in simplest form.
$$5\frac{1}{3} \cdot 2\frac{3}{8}$$

27. What is the reciprocal of 16?

28. Find the quotient. Write your answer as a mixed number in simplest form.
$$\frac{11}{5} \div \frac{8}{24}$$

29. Describe the first step when dividing two mixed numbers.

30. Evaluate the expression below if $y = 4\frac{1}{5}$.
$$4\frac{4}{5} + y$$

31. Solve the equation. $4\frac{2}{3}k = 3\frac{1}{2}$

32. A leaky faucet drips once every 10 seconds. How many times does the faucet drip in a 24-hour day?

33. Which of the following would not be used to measure length?
meters, ounces, inches, feet

34. Complete the statement.
184 pt = __?__ gal

35. Subtract.
$$\begin{array}{r} 6 \text{ gal } 1 \text{ qt} \\ - 2 \text{ gal } 3 \text{ qt} \\ \hline \end{array}$$

36. Cindy-Lu is making pancakes for her entire family. The recipe calls for 2 cups of milk. The store only sells milk by the gallon. How many gallons of milk does she need to buy if she wants to make the recipe 9 times?

Quarter 2 Test

Chapters 4–6

Form B

1. Use mental math to determine if 1,923 is divisible by 3.

2. Use a factor tree to find the prime factorization of 280. Write your answer using exponents.

3. Find the GCF of 32, 48, and 112.

4. If you were to plot the fractions $\frac{2}{5}$ and $\frac{6}{15}$ on the same number line, where would they be in relation to each other?

5. Write a fraction with a denominator of 65 that is equivalent to $\frac{2}{5}$.

6. Write $\frac{52}{10}$ as a mixed number.

7. Find the LCM of 24 and 84.

8. Order the mixed numbers from least to greatest.
$5\frac{2}{5}, 5\frac{1}{2}, 5\frac{4}{11}$

9. Fill in the __?__ with $<$, $>$, or $=$.
$\frac{27}{7}$ __?__ $3\frac{5}{7}$

10. Write 0.275 as a fraction in simplest form.

11. Write $11\frac{3}{25}$ as a decimal.

12. Write nine and three fifths as a decimal.

13. The sum of two decimals is 1.8. One of the decimals is twice the other. What are the two decimals?

14. Round $7\frac{14}{29}$ to the nearest whole number.

15. Estimate $19\frac{1}{7} - 6\frac{5}{8}$ by first rounding to the nearest whole number.

16. Add. Write your answer in simplest form.
$\frac{2}{15} + \frac{7}{15} - \frac{6}{15}$

17. Explain how you would add the fractions $\frac{1}{3}$ and $\frac{1}{6}$.

18. Sandy walked $3\frac{1}{2}$ miles on Saturday and $2\frac{5}{8}$ on Sunday. How many miles did she walk during the weekend?

19. Add. Write your answer in simplest form.
$9\frac{2}{5} + 7\frac{1}{3} + 4\frac{11}{15}$

20. There are two jump ropes hanging on a peg. The first rope is $3\frac{3}{4}$ feet long and the second is $4\frac{1}{8}$ feet long. How much longer is the second rope?

21. What is the first step in solving the equation $x - 3\frac{1}{4} = 5$?

22. Solve the equation. Write your answer in simplest form.

$x + 2\frac{1}{2} = 5\frac{1}{9}$

23. Find the elapsed time from 2:48 P.M. to 4:06 P.M.

24. Which product is NOT equal to the others?

A. $\frac{3}{2} \cdot \frac{10}{18}$　**B.** $\frac{2}{1} \cdot \frac{3}{5}$　**C.** $\frac{1}{2} \cdot \frac{5}{3}$　**D.** $\frac{1}{5} \cdot \frac{25}{6}$

25. A chocolate cake has a total of about 2,400 calories. The pie is divided into 12 equal slices. Write an expression using a fraction to calculate the number of calories in each slice. Then calculate the number of calories in each slice.

26. Find the product. Write your answer as a mixed number in simplest form.

$10\frac{1}{2} \cdot 4\frac{3}{7}$

27. What is the reciprocal of 24?

28. Find the quotient. Write your answer in simplest form.

$\frac{16}{3} \div \frac{4}{21}$

29. Describe the first step when multiplying two mixed numbers.

30. Evaluate the expression for $p = 3\frac{1}{6}$.

$1\frac{4}{15} \div p$

31. Solve the equation. $3\frac{1}{5}p = 2\frac{2}{3}$

32. The average person takes a breath once every 5 seconds. How many breaths does an average person take in 16 hours?

33. Which of the following would not be used to measure capacity?

pints, quarts, gallons, yards

34. Complete the statement.

224 oz = ___?___ qt

35. Add.

```
  2 gal  3 qt
+ 4 gal  2 qt
```

36. Leah lives down the street from her best friend. Leah's mom told her that her friend's house is approximately 880 yards away. About how many miles away is Leah's friend's house?

Quarter 2 Test

Form D

Chapters 4–6

1. Use mental math to determine whether 22,645 is divisible by 9.

2. Use a factor tree to find the prime factorization of 120. Write your answer using exponents.

3. Find the GCF of 12, 16, and 36.

4. If you were to plot the fractions $\frac{3}{12}$ and $\frac{1}{4}$ on the same number line, where would they be in relation to each other?

5. Write a fraction with a denominator of 18 that is equivalent to $\frac{2}{3}$.

6. Write $\frac{44}{6}$ as a mixed number.

7. Find the LCM of 10 and 6.

8. Order the mixed numbers from least to greatest.
   $3\frac{4}{7}, 3\frac{8}{15}, 3\frac{1}{2}$

9. Fill in the __?__ with $<, >$, or $=$.
   $\frac{23}{9}$ __?__ $2\frac{10}{18}$

10. Write 0.45 as a fraction in simplest form.

11. Write $6\frac{7}{20}$ as a decimal.

12. Round $11\frac{7}{12}$ to the nearest whole number.

13. Estimate $7\frac{4}{5} + 9\frac{1}{12}$ by first rounding to the nearest whole number.

14. Add. Write your answer in simplest form.
    $\frac{3}{20} + \frac{7}{20} - \frac{2}{20}$

15. Explain how you would add the fractions $\frac{1}{2}$ and $\frac{3}{4}$.

16. Sean rode his bicycle $4\frac{1}{4}$ miles on Saturday and $5\frac{7}{8}$ miles on Sunday. How many miles did he ride during the weekend?

17. There are two boards leaning against the wall. The first board is $3\frac{5}{8}$ meters long and the second is $4\frac{1}{4}$ meters long. How much longer is the second board?

18. What is the first step in solving the equation $x + 1\frac{5}{6} = 5$?

19. Find the elapsed time from 8:35 A.M. to 10:15 A.M.

20. A chocolate pie has a total of about 2,200 calories. The pie is divided into 8 equal slices. Write an expression using a fraction to calculate the number of calories in each slice. Then calculate the number of calories in each slice.

21. Find the product. Write your answer as a mixed number in simplest form.

$5\frac{1}{3} \cdot 2\frac{3}{8}$

22. What is the reciprocal of 16?

23. Find the quotient. Write your answer as a mixed number in simplest form.

$\frac{11}{5} \div \frac{8}{24}$

24. Describe the first step when dividing two mixed numbers.

25. Evaluate the expression below if $y = 4\frac{1}{5}$.

$4\frac{4}{5} + y$

26. Which of the following would not be used to measure length?

meters, ounces, inches, feet

27. Subtract.

$$\begin{array}{r} 6 \text{ gal } 1 \text{ qt} \\ - 2 \text{ gal } 3 \text{ qt} \\ \hline \end{array}$$

Quarter 2 Test

Chapters 4–6

Form E

1. Use mental math to determine if 1,923 is divisible by 3.

2. Use a factor tree to find the prime factorization of 280. Write your answer using exponents.

3. Find the GCF of 12, 18, and 42.

4. If you were to plot the fractions $\frac{2}{5}$ and $\frac{6}{15}$ on the same number line, where would they be in relation to each other?

5. Write a fraction with a denominator of 65 that is equivalent to $\frac{2}{5}$.

6. Write $\frac{52}{10}$ as a mixed number.

7. Find the LCM of 8 and 14.

8. Order the mixed numbers from least to greatest.

$5\frac{2}{5}, 5\frac{1}{2}, 5\frac{4}{11}$

9. Fill in the __?__ with $<, >$, or $=$.

$\frac{27}{7}$ __?__ $3\frac{5}{7}$

10. Write 0.36 as a fraction in simplest form.

11. Write $11\frac{3}{25}$ as a decimal.

12. Round $7\frac{14}{29}$ to the nearest whole number.

13. Estimate $19\frac{1}{7} - 6\frac{5}{8}$ by first rounding to the nearest whole number.

14. Add. Write your answer in simplest form.

$\frac{2}{15} + \frac{7}{15} - \frac{6}{15}$

15. Explain how you would add the fractions $\frac{1}{3}$ and $\frac{1}{6}$.

16. Sandy walked $3\frac{1}{2}$ miles on Saturday and $2\frac{5}{8}$ on Sunday. How many miles did she walk during the weekend?

17. There are two jump ropes hanging on a peg. The first rope is $3\frac{3}{4}$ feet long and the second is $4\frac{1}{8}$ feet long. How much longer is the second rope?

18. What is the first step in solving the equation $x - 3\frac{1}{4} = 5$?

19. Find the elapsed time from 2:48 P.M. to 4:06 P.M.

20. A chocolate cake has a total of about 2,400 calories. The cake is divided into 12 equal slices. Write an expression using a fraction to calculate the number of calories in each slice. Then calculate the number of calories in each slice.

21. Find the product. Write your answer as a mixed number in simplest form.

$$10\frac{1}{2} \cdot 4\frac{3}{7}$$

22. What is the reciprocal of 24?

23. Find the quotient. Write your answer in simplest form.

$$\frac{16}{3} \div \frac{4}{21}$$

24. Describe the first step when multiplying two mixed numbers.

25. Evaluate the expression for $p = 3\frac{1}{6}$.

$$1\frac{4}{15} \div p$$

26. Which of the following would not be used to measure capacity?

pints, quarts, gallons, yards

27. Add.

$$\begin{array}{r} 2 \text{ gal } 3 \text{ qt} \\ + \ 4 \text{ gal } 2 \text{ qt} \\ \hline \end{array}$$

Quarter 3 Test

Form A

Chapters 7–9

1. There are 24 horses on a ranch. If $\frac{3}{8}$ of the horses on the ranch are palominos, how many are palominos?

2. If 14% of the 200 students in a school swim on the school swim team, how many students swim on the team?

3. A jar contains 14 red marbles, 20 yellow marbles, and 6 green marbles. Find the ratio of green marbles to all of the marbles. Write the ratio in simplest form.

4. Write 64% as a fraction in simplest form and as a decimal.

5. Write $\frac{1}{8}$ as a decimal and as a percent. Round to the nearest whole percent.

6. Do the ratios $\frac{10}{15}$ and $\frac{2}{5}$ form a proportion? Explain.

7. You are making a model of a 96-ft-tall roller coaster loop. Your scale is 1 inch : 6 feet. Find the height of your model.

8. Which is the better buy? Explain your answer.
   60 oz of Brand A cat food priced at $6.00
   50 oz of Brand Z cat food priced at $5.50

9. Use the circle graph below to determine what percent of students do NOT walk *or* take the bus to school.

Transportation to School

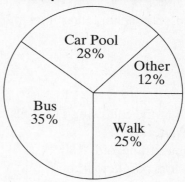

10. Which of the following has two endpoints? line, ray, segment, point

Use the diagram below for Exercises 11–13.

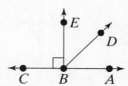

11. Which point is the vertex of $\angle CBD$?

12. Name an acute angle.

13. $m\angle ABD + m\angle DBE = m\angle \underline{\ ?\ }$

14. Find the complement of an angle with measure 42°.

15. An isosceles triangle has how many equal sides?

16. Which of the following polygons is not a quadrilateral?
rhombus, trapezoid,
pentagon, parallelogram

17. If triangle *JKL* is congruent to triangle *PQR*, which side of triangle *PQR* is congruent to $\overline{JL}$?

18. Describe four lines of symmetry that can be drawn through a square.

19. A ray is pointed straight down. The ray is rotated 90° counterclockwise. Is the ray now pointed to the left or to the right?

20. Fill in the __?__ with <, >, or =.
100 mm __?__ 10 cm

21. Convert 460 meters to kilometers.

22. The area of a parallelogram is 25 square feet. If the length of the base is 10 feet, what is the height of the parallelogram?

23. Find the area of the triangle.

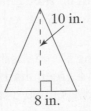

24. A tennis ball is attached to the end of a rope that is 3 feet long. If you spin the ball around in a circle 5 times, how far does it travel?

25. Find the area of a circle whose circumference is 12π ft. Write your answer in terms of π.

26. What is another name for a rectangular prism whose faces and bases are all the same shape and size?

27. Find the surface area of the figure below.

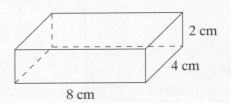

28. The base of a cylinder has a diameter of 6.2 cm. The cylinder is 18 cm tall. What is the volume of the cylinder? Use 3.14 for π.

Quarter 3 Test

Chapters 7–9

Form B

1. There are 32 horses on a ranch. If $\frac{5}{8}$ of the horses on the ranch are bays, how many are bays?

2. There are 260 students in a school. If 143 of them play a musical instrument, what percent of the students play a musical instrument?

3. A jar contains 14 red marbles, 20 yellow marbles, and 6 green marbles. Find the ratio of green marbles to red marbles. Write the ratio in simplest form.

4. Write 88% as a fraction in simplest form and as a decimal.

5. Write $\frac{5}{6}$ as a decimal and as a percent. Round to the nearest whole percent.

6. Do the ratios $\frac{18}{15}$ and $\frac{5}{6}$ form a proportion? Explain.

7. You are making a model of a giant water park swing. The structure stands 180 feet tall. Your scale is 1 inch : 6 feet. Find the height of your model.

8. Which is the better buy? Explain your answer.
   48 ounces of juice for $2.40
   32 ounces of juice for $1.92

9. Use the circle graph below to determine what percent of students do NOT carpool *or* take the bus to school.

Transportation to School

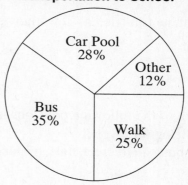

10. Which of the following has only one endpoint? line, ray, segment, point

Use the diagram below for Exercises 11–13.

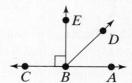

11. Point *B* is the _____ of $\angle ABD$.

12. Name an obtuse angle.

13. $m\angle CBE + m\angle EBD = m\angle\ \underline{\ ?\ }$

14. Find the supplement of an angle with measure 42°.

15. A scalene triangle has how many equal sides?

16. Which of the following polygons is not a parallelogram?
rhombus, square, rectangle, trapezoid

17. If triangle *NOP* is congruent to triangle *STU,* which angle of triangle *STU* is congruent to angle *P*?

18. Describe three lines of symmetry that can be drawn through an equilateral triangle.

19. A ray is pointed straight down. The ray is reflected across a horizontal line. Is the ray now pointed up, down, to the left, or to the right?

20. Fill in the __?__ with <, >, or =.
10,000 g __?__ 100 kg

21. Convert 212 milliliters to liters.

22. The area of a parallelogram is 24 square meters. If the height of the parallelogram is 16 meters, what is the length of the base?

23. Find the area of the triangle.

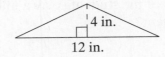

24. The Ferris wheel at the county fair is 30 feet tall. If a person rides the Ferris wheel around 4 times, how far has he traveled?

25. Find the area of a circle whose circumference is 22π m. Write your answer in terms of π.

26. How many edges does a square pyramid have?

27. Find the surface area of the figure below.

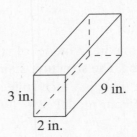

28. The base of a cylinder has a diameter of 8.6 in. The cylinder is 12 in. tall. What is the volume of the cylinder? Use 3.14 for π.

Quarter 3 Test

Form D

Chapters 7–9

1. Solve the proportion. $\frac{3}{8} = \frac{x}{24}$

2. If 14% of the 200 students in a school swim on the school swim team, how many students swim on the team?

3. A jar contains 8 red marbles, 12 yellow marbles, and 5 green marbles. Find the ratio of green marbles to all of the marbles. Write the ratio in simplest form.

4. Write 15% as a decimal.

5. Write $\frac{1}{5}$ as a percent.

6. Do the ratios $\frac{10}{15}$ and $\frac{2}{5}$ form a proportion? Explain.

7. You are making a model of a roller coaster loop. The loop is 96 feet tall. Your scale is 1 inch : 3 feet. Find the height of your model.

8. Which is the better buy? Explain your answer.
   60 oz of Brand A cat food priced at $6.00
   50 oz of Brand Z cat food priced at $5.50

9. Use the circle graph below to determine what percent of students do NOT walk *or* take the bus to school.

Transportation to School

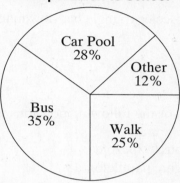

10. Which of the following has two endpoints?
    line, ray, segment, point

Use the diagram below for Exercises 11–13.

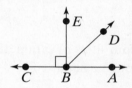

11. Which point is the vertex of $\angle CBD$?

12. Name an acute angle.

13. $m\angle ABD + m\angle DBE = m\angle \underline{\ ?\ }$

14. Find the complement of an angle with measure 40°.

15. An isosceles triangle has how many equal sides?

16. Which of the following polygons is not a quadrilateral?
rhombus, trapezoid,
pentagon, parallelogram

17. If triangle *JKL* is congruent to triangle *PQR*, which side of triangle *PQR* is congruent to $\overline{JL}$?

18. Describe four lines of symmetry that can be drawn through a square.

19. A ray is pointed straight down. The ray is rotated 90° counterclockwise. Is the ray now pointed to the left or to the right?

20. Convert 5,800 meters to kilometers.

21. Find the area of a parallelogram whose base is 5 cm and whose height is 7 cm.

22. Find the circumference of a circle whose diameter is 4 inches. Use 3.14 for π.

23. Find the area of the triangle.

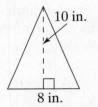

24. Find the area of a circle whose radius is 10 ft. Use 3.14 for π.

25. What is another name for a rectangular prism whose faces and bases are all the same shape and size?

26. Find the surface area of the figure below.

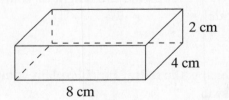

27. The base of a cylinder has a diameter of 10 cm. The cylinder is 7 cm tall. What is the volume of the cylinder? Use 3.14 for π.

Quarter 3 Test

Form E

Chapters 7–9

1. Solve the proportion. $\frac{5}{8} = \frac{x}{32}$

2. There are 260 students in a school. If 143 of them play a musical instrument, what percent of the students play a musical instrument?

3. A jar contains 10 red marbles, 15 yellow marbles, and 6 green marbles. Find the ratio of green marbles to red marbles. Write the ratio in simplest form.

4. Write 38% as a decimal.

5. Write $\frac{1}{4}$ as a percent.

6. Do the ratios $\frac{12}{15}$ and $\frac{3}{4}$ form a proportion? Explain.

7. You are making a model of a giant water park swing. The structure stands 180 feet tall. Your scale is 1 inch : 6 feet. Find the height of your model.

8. Which is the better buy? Explain your answer.
   48 ounces of juice for $2.40
   32 ounces of juice for $1.92

9. Use the circle graph below to determine what percent of students do NOT carpool *or* take the bus to school.

Transportation to School

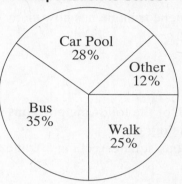

10. Which of the following has only one endpoint? line, ray, segment, point

Use the diagram below for Exercises 11–13.

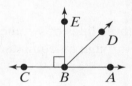

11. Point *B* is the _____ of ∠*ABD*.

12. Name an obtuse angle.

13. $m\angle CBE + m\angle EBD = m\angle\ \underline{\ ?\ }$

14. Find the supplement of an angle with measure 50°.

15. A scalene triangle has how many equal sides?

16. Which of the following polygons is not a parallelogram?
rhombus, square, rectangle, trapezoid

17. If triangle *NOP* is congruent to triangle *STU,* which angle of triangle *STU* is congruent to angle *P*?

18. Describe three lines of symmetry that can be drawn through an equilateral triangle.

19. A ray is pointed straight down. The ray is reflected across a horizontal line. Is the ray now pointed up, down, to the left, or to the right?

20. Convert 2,100 milliliters to liters.

21. Find the area of a parallelogram whose base is 8 cm and whose height is 5 cm.

22. Find the circumference of a circle whose diameter is 8 inches. Use 3.14 for π.

23. Find the area of the triangle.

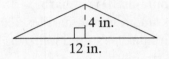

24. Find the area of a circle whose radius is 3 m. Use 3.14 for π.

25. How many edges does a square pyramid have?

26. Find the surface area of the figure below.

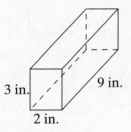

27. The base of a cylinder has a diameter of 4 in. The cylinder is 10 in. tall. What is the volume of the cylinder? Use 3.14 for π.

Quarter 4 Test

Form A

Chapters 10–12

1. Find the value of $|-12| + |3|$.

2. Order from least to greatest.
$-6, 3, 1, -1, -9$

3. Add. $-6 + 10$

4. Add. $-15 + (-20)$

5. Subtract. $-14 - (-6)$

6. Subtract. $12.5 - (-2.5) - 2$

7. Multiply. $8 \times (-2) \times (-0.5) \times (-3)$

8. Which of the following is NOT equal to -4?
 A. $\frac{(-8)}{2}$ **B.** $(-2) \cdot (-2)$ **C.** $\frac{20}{(-5)}$

Use the coordinate plane below for Exercises 9 and 10. Find the coordinates of each point.

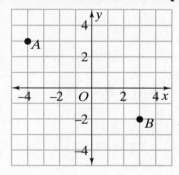

9. Point A

10. Point B

11. At midnight, the temperature was $-14°F$. By noon, it had risen $26°F$. What was the temperature at noon?

12. Fill in the _?_ for the function that is graphed below.
$y = x +$ _?_

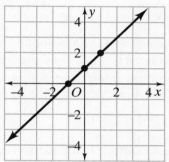

13. If the x-coordinates of two points are the same, do the points form a horizontal or vertical line?

14. Three points are plotted on a coordinate graph. The three points are $(-2, 5)$, $(4, 5)$, and $(-2, -1)$. If you wanted to graph a square, what fourth point would you need to plot?

15. What polygon is formed by the points?
$(-1, 2), (-2, -3), (2, 2), (5, -3)$

16. Fill in the _?_ to complete the function box.

x	y
4	2
6	3
8	_?_

17. There are three mystery books, two science fiction books, and four nonfiction books on a shelf. If you choose a book at random, what is the probability that you will choose a nonfiction book?

18. If the probability that an event will happen is $\frac{11}{20}$, what is the probability that the event will NOT happen?

19. A football quarterback completes 9 out of 14 passes. Find the experimental probability of the quarterback completing a pass.

20. The probability that a baseball team will win a game is 60%. If they play 45 games in a season, how many games should they expect to win?

21. Use the Counting Principle to find the probability of rolling two 3's when you roll a number cube twice.

22. A spinner is divided into four equal sections. Two of the sections are red, one is blue, and one is yellow. You spin the spinner three times. What is the probability that you will get red, then blue, then red again?

23. Fill in the __?__.
If A and B are independent events, then $P(A, \text{then } B) = P(A)$ __?__ $P(B)$

24. Decide whether the events are independent.

You pick a card at random from a deck and keep it. Your partner picks one after you.

25. A bag contains 4 red, 6 blue, and 1 white chip. You draw a chip at random from the bag and replace it. Then you draw a second chip. What is the probability of getting a blue chip, then a red one?

26. Describe how you would solve $2x + 5 = 17$.

27. Solve. $45 = 30 + 5x$

28. Write an inequality for the situation.

There are at least 200 people waiting in line for the concert.

29. Write an inequality for the graph.

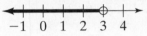

30. Write an inequality for the sentence. Then solve the inequality.

A number increased by 6 is less than 15.

31. Solve. $\frac{w}{3} - 1 \geq 4$

32. Which of the following is NOT a rational number?
$\frac{4}{17}$ $\sqrt{30}$ $9.171717\ldots$ $\sqrt{36}$

33. Between which consecutive whole numbers does $\sqrt{300}$ lie?

34. Explain why $\sqrt{16} + \sqrt{9} \neq \sqrt{25}$.

35. Find the missing side length for the right triangle whose dimensions are given. Round your answer to the nearest tenth.
$a = 12, b = 20, c = ?$

Quarter 4 Test

Form B

Chapters 10–12

1. Find the value of $|7| + |-14|$.

2. Order from least to greatest.
   $5, -17, 0, 7, -12$

3. Add. $-20 + 14$

4. Add. $-5 + (-9)$

5. Subtract. $-23 - (-11)$

6. Subtract. $17.6 - (-2.4) - 5$

7. Multiply. $12 \times (-2) \times (-0.5) \times (-5)$

8. Which of the following is NOT equal to -6?
   A. $\dfrac{(-12)}{2}$ B. $(-2) \cdot (3)$ C. $\dfrac{(-30)}{(-5)}$

Use the coordinate plane below for Exercises 9 and 10. Find the coordinates of each point.

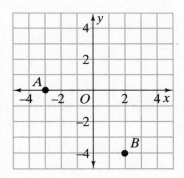

9. Point A

10. Point B

11. At 5:00 P.M., the temperature was 22°F. By midnight, it had fallen 30°. What was the temperature at midnight?

12. Fill in the ? for the function that is graphed below.
    $y = x - $?

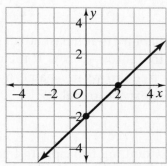

13. If the y-coordinates of two points are the same, do the points form a horizontal or vertical line?

14. Three points are plotted on a coordinate graph. The three points are $(-3, 0)$, $(5, 0)$, and $(5, 4)$. If you wanted to graph a rectangle, what fourth point would you need to plot?

15. What polygon is formed by the points? $(-3, -2), (2, -2), (0, 2), (5, 2)$

16. Fill in the ? to complete the function box.

x	y
2	?
4	-2
6	-3

17. A box contains 5 baseball cards, 6 basketball cards, and 8 football cards. If you choose a card at random from the box, what is the probability that you will get a basketball card?

18. If the probability that an event will happen is 0.47, what is the probability that the event will NOT happen?

19. A hockey goalie blocks 5 out of 7 shots. Find the experimental probability of the goalie blocking a shot.

20. The probability that a basketball player will make a free throw is 75%. If the player shoots 8 free throws in a game, how many should he expect to make?

21. Use the Counting Principle to find the probability of getting three tails if you flip a coin three times.

22. A spinner is divided into five equal sections. Three of the sections are red, one is blue, and one is green. You spin the spinner three times. What is the probability that you will get blue, then red, then green?

23. Fill in the ? .

If A and B are independent events, then $P(A \text{ and } B) = P(A)$ _?_ $P(B)$

24. Decide whether the events are independent.

You spin a colored spinner. Your partner spins it after you.

25. A bag contains 3 red, 5 blue, and 1 black chip. You draw a chip at random from the bag and replace it. Then you draw a second chip. What is the probability of getting a blue chip, then a black one?

26. Describe how you would solve $\frac{x}{3} + 11 = 20$.

27. Solve. $28 = 4 + 12h$

28. Write an inequality for the situation. There are at most 50 people waiting in the movie theater.

29. Write an inequality for the graph.

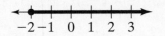

30. Write an inequality for the sentence. Then solve the inequality.

A number decreased by 12 is greater than or equal to 15.

31. Solve. $\frac{t}{9} + 5 < 7$

32. Which of the following is NOT a rational number?

$5.272727\ldots$ $\qquad \sqrt{25} \qquad \frac{2}{5} \qquad \sqrt{20}$

33. Between which consecutive whole numbers does $\sqrt{500}$ lie?

34. Explain why $\sqrt{36} + \sqrt{64} \neq \sqrt{100}$.

35. Find the missing side length for the right triangle whose dimensions are given. Round your answer to the nearest tenth.
$a = 14, b = 22, c = ?$

Quarter 4 Test

Form D

Chapters 10–12

1. Find the value of $|-12| + |3|$.

2. Order from least to greatest.
   $-6, 3, 1, -1, -9$

3. Add. $-15 + (-20)$

4. Subtract. $-14 - (-6)$

5. Multiply. $8 \times (-2) \times (-0.5) \times (-3)$

6. Which of the following is NOT equal to -4?
   A. $\frac{(-8)}{2}$ **B.** $(-2) \cdot (-2)$ **C.** $\frac{20}{(-5)}$

**Use the coordinate plane below for Exercises 9–10.
Find the coordinates of each point.**

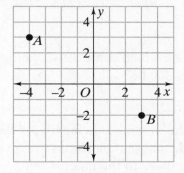

7. Point A

8. Point B

9. At midnight, the temperature was $-14°F$. By noon, it had risen $26°F$. What was the temperature at noon?

10. Fill in the __?__ for the function that is graphed below.
    $y = x + $ __?__

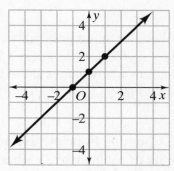

11. If the x-coordinates of two points are the same, do the points form a horizontal or vertical line?

12. Three points are plotted on a coordinate graph. The three points are $(-2, 5)$, $(4, 5)$, and $(-2, -1)$. If you wanted to graph a square, what fourth point would you need to plot?

13. Fill in the __?__ to complete the function box.

x	y
4	7
6	8
8	?

14. There are three mystery books, two science fiction books, and four nonfiction books on a shelf. If you choose a book at random, what is the probability that you will choose a nonfiction book?

15. If the probability that an event will happen is $\frac{11}{20}$, what is the probability that the event will NOT happen?

16. A football quarterback completes 9 out of 14 passes. Find the experimental probability of the quarterback completing a pass.

17. The probability that a baseball team will win a game is 60%. If they play 45 games in a season, how many games should they expect to win?

18. Use the Counting Principle to find the probability of rolling two 3's when you roll a number cube twice.

19. Decide whether the events are independent.

You pick a card at random from a deck and keep it. Your partner picks one after you.

20. A bag contains 4 red, 6 blue, and 1 white chip. You draw a chip at random from the bag and replace it. Then you draw a second chip. What is the probability of getting a blue chip, then a red one?

21. Solve. $45 = 30 + 5x$

22. Write an inequality for the graph.

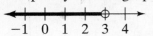

23. Write an inequality for the sentence. Then solve the inequality.

A number increased by 6 is less than 15.

24. Solve. $\frac{w}{3} - 1 \geq 4$

25. Which of the following is NOT a rational number?

$\frac{4}{17}$ $\sqrt{30}$ $9.171717\ldots$ $\sqrt{36}$

26. Between which consecutive whole numbers does $\sqrt{300}$ lie?

27. Find the missing side length for the right triangle whose dimensions are given. Round your answer to the nearest tenth.
$a = 8, b = 6, c = ?$

Quarter 4 Test
Chapters 10–12

Form E

1. Find the value of $|7| + |-14|$.

2. Order from least to greatest.
   $5, -17, 0, 7, -12$

3. Add. $-5 + (-9)$

4. Subtract. $-23 - (-11)$

5. Multiply. $12 \times (-2) \times (-0.5) \times (-5)$

6. Which of the following is NOT equal to -6?
   A. $\dfrac{(-12)}{2}$ **B.** $(-2) \cdot (3)$ **C.** $\dfrac{(-30)}{(-5)}$

Use the coordinate plane below for Exercises 9–10. Find the coordinates of each point.

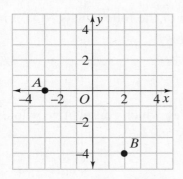

7. Point A

8. Point B

9. At 5:00 P.M., the temperature was 22°F. By midnight, it had fallen 30°. What was the temperature at midnight?

10. Fill in the _?_ for the function that is graphed below.
    $y = x - \underline{\ ?\ }$

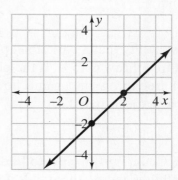

11. If the y-coordinates of two points are the same, do the points form a horizontal or vertical line?

12. Three points are plotted on a coordinate graph. The three points are $(-3, 0)$, $(5, 0)$, and $(5, 4)$. If you wanted to graph a rectangle, what fourth point would you need to plot?

13. Fill in the _?_ to complete the function box.

x	y
3	?
4	2
5	3

14. A box contains 5 baseball cards, 6 basketball cards, and 8 football cards. If you choose a card at random from the box, what is the probability that you will get a basketball card?

15. If the probability that an event will happen is 0.47, what is the probability that the event will NOT happen?

16. A hockey goalie blocks 5 out of 7 shots. Find the experimental probability of the goalie blocking a shot.

17. The probability that a basketball player will make a free throw is 75%. If the player shoots 8 free throws in a game, how many should he expect to make?

18. Use the Counting Principle to find the probability of getting three tails if you flip a coin three times.

19. Decide whether the events are independent.

You spin a colored spinner. Your partner spins it after you.

20. A bag contains 3 red, 5 blue, and 1 black chip. You draw a chip at random from the bag and replace it. Then you draw a second chip. What is the probability of getting a blue chip, then a black one?

21. Solve. $28 = 4 + 12h$

22. Write an inequality for the graph.

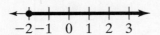

23. Write an inequality for the sentence. Then solve the inequality.

A number decreased by 12 is greater than or equal to 15.

24. Solve. $\frac{t}{9} + 5 < 7$

25. Which of the following is NOT a rational number?

5.272727 . . . $\sqrt{25}$ $\frac{2}{5}$ $\sqrt{20}$

26. Between which consecutive whole numbers does $\sqrt{500}$ lie?

27. Find the missing side length for the right triangle whose dimensions are given. Round your answer to the nearest tenth.
$a = 9, b = 12, c = ?$

Mid-Course Test

Chapter 1–6

Form A

1. Write ten and forty-six thousandths in standard form.

2. Order the decimals from least to greatest.
   4.3, 4.19, 4.299, 4.2, 3.99

3. Round 67.32 to the tens place.

4. Find the sum. $1.46 + 9.3 + 0.7$

5. A baseball game begins at 8:00 P.M. It takes 45 minutes to get there. When should you leave for the game if you want to arrive one hour early?

6. Explain how you would use mental math to divide 7.6 by 100.

7. Evaluate the expression.
   $12.1 \div (11 \times 11) + 0.9$

8. Write a rule to describe the number pattern.
   5, 15, 45, 135, . . .

9. Evaluate the expression for the given values.
   $3x - 7y$ for $x = 12$ and $y = 3$

10. Solve. $x + 1.6 = 3$

11. Explain why the number 3 is NOT a solution to the equation $12x = 30$.

12. Write $2 \times 2 \times 2 \times p \times p \times p \times p \times p$ using exponents.

13. Evaluate. $(3^2 - 8)^2 + 5^2$

14. Rewrite $4(f + 3)$ using the Distributive Property.

15. Write an expression equivalent to $(15 \cdot 10) + (15 \cdot 10)$

16. What kind of numbers are NOT divisible by two?

17. The prime factorization of a number is $2 \times 2 \times 3 \times 5 \times 5$. What is the number?

18. The GCF of 28 and some other number is 7. What are the two least possible values for the other number?

19. What fraction is plotted on the number line?

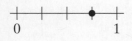

20. Fill in the __?__ with $<, >,$ or $=$.
$\frac{5}{11}$ __?__ $\frac{1}{2}$

21. Write an improper fraction with a denominator of 12 that is equivalent to two and one fourth.

22. The prime factorizations of two numbers are $2 \times 2 \times 2 \times 3 \times 7$ and $2 \times 2 \times 3 \times 5$. What is the LCM of the two numbers?

23. Tom ran $3\frac{1}{5}$ miles. John ran $3\frac{3}{20}$ miles. Who ran farther?

24. Describe how to convert 0.45 to a fraction in simplest terms. Write the fraction.

25. Round $22\frac{3}{8}$ in. to the nearest half inch.

26. $\frac{11}{23}$ of your class are girls. What fraction of the class is boys?

Mid-Course Test (continued)

Form A

Chapters 1–6

27. Write the difference in simplest form.
$\frac{2}{3} - \frac{1}{12} - \frac{1}{4}$

28. Write the sum in simplest form.
$11\frac{13}{14} + 3\frac{1}{7}$

29. Write the difference in simplest form.
$25\frac{1}{10} - 12\frac{4}{5}$

30. Solve. Write your answer in simplest form.
$15\frac{1}{3} = n + 4\frac{5}{6}$

31. You are going on a trip by plane. Your first flight arrives at 11:20 A.M. Your connection flight departs at 1:10 P.M. How long do you have to wait at the airport between flights?

32. Evaluate $30n$ for $n = \frac{14}{15}$.

33. A newborn kitten is about $3\frac{1}{2}$ inches long. The mother cat is 4 times as long as the baby. How long is the mother?

34. Find the quotient. Write your answer in simplest form.
$\frac{1}{2} \div \frac{11}{12}$

35. A standard 2-by-4 board is 8 feet long. How many $1\frac{1}{2}$-foot stakes can you make out of one standard 2-by-4? How much wood will you have left over?

36. Solve. $\frac{7}{3}b = 2\frac{1}{3}$

37. A grandfather clock chimes every $\frac{1}{4}$ of an hour. How many times does it chime in a week?

38. What unit of measurement would you most likely use to measure the weight of a car?

39. Complete the statement.
    504 h = __?__ weeks

40. Make a line plot of the following test scores: 84, 88, 90, 94, 100, 88, 90, 90, 94

41. Find the range for the data set in Exercise 40.

42. Find the mode for the data set in Exercise 40.

43. Which type of data display, a bar graph or a line graph, is more appropriate for displaying the following data? Explain.

    Sales at a gift shop:

    January: $20,000

    February: $16,000

    March: $15,000

    April: $16,500

Use the following spreadsheet for Exercises 44 and 45.

	A	B	C	D
		Book Sales ($)	Music Sales ($)	Total Sales ($)
1	Date			
2	11-02-06	554	683	
3	11-03-06	679	650	

44. What is the value in cell C2?

45. Write the formula for cell D3.

46. Which measurement, the mean or the median, more accurately describes the data in the following data display?

    ```
    1 | 94
    2 | 26 30 31 32
    3 | 68 69
    ```

    Key: 1 | 94 means 194.

Mid-Course Test

Chapters 1–6

Form B

1. Write one hundred, six and eight hundredths in standard form.

2. Order the decimals from least to greatest.
6.09, 6.6, 6.2, 6.1, 6.59

3. Round 124.83 to the ones place.

4. Find the difference. $29.8 - 6.38$

5. A football game begins at 2:00 P.M. It takes 45 minutes to get there. When should you leave for the game if you want to arrive a half hour early?

6. Explain how you would use mental math to multiply 32.6 by 100.

7. Evaluate the expression.
$2.5 \div (5 \times 5) + 2.9$

8. Write a rule to describe the number pattern.
10, 30, 50, 70, . . .

9. Evaluate the expression for the given values.
$9m + n$ for $m = 4$ and $n = 15$

10. Solve. $3.1 - x = 2$

11. Explain why the number 15 is NOT a solution to the equation $p \div 3 = 6$.

12. Write $3 \times 3 \times 3 \times 3 \times k \times k$ using exponents.

13. Evaluate. $4^2 - (5^2 - 23)$

14. Rewrite $(7 + m) \cdot 3$ using the Distributive Property.

15. Write an expression that is equivalent to $(45 \cdot 10) + (45 \cdot 2)$.

16. How do you know when a number is divisible by five?

17. The prime factorization of a number is $2 \times 3 \times 3 \times 3 \times 7$. What is the number?

18. The GCF of 36 and some other number is 9. What are the two least possible values for the other number?

19. What fraction is plotted on the number line?

20. Fill in the __?__ with $<$, $>$, or $=$.

$\frac{15}{16}$ __?__ $\frac{7}{8}$

21. Write an improper fraction with a denominator of 6 that is equivalent to three and one half.

22. The prime factorizations of two numbers are $2 \times 3 \times 7$ and $2 \times 2 \times 3 \times 5$. What is the LCM of the two numbers?

23. Sally ran $2\frac{4}{5}$ miles. John ran $2\frac{6}{7}$ miles. Who ran farther?

24. Describe how to convert 0.32 to a fraction in simplest terms. Write the fraction.

25. Round $17\frac{3}{16}$ in. to the nearest half inch.

26. $\frac{7}{25}$ of your class are in the school play. What fraction of the class is not in the play?

Mid-Course Test (continued)

Form B

Chapters 1–6

27. Write the sum in simplest form.
$\frac{1}{2} + \frac{3}{16} + \frac{1}{8}$

28. Write the sum in simplest form.
$17\frac{11}{12} + 3\frac{2}{3}$

29. Write the difference in simplest form.
$18\frac{2}{15} - 9\frac{4}{5}$

30. Solve. Write your answer in simplest form.
$5\frac{1}{4} = n - 15\frac{7}{8}$

31. You are planning on going to two baseball games on Saturday. The first game is over at 2:50 P.M. The second game begins at 3:45 P.M. How long between games do you have to wait?

32. Evaluate $36m$ for $m = \frac{11}{12}$.

33. A newborn beagle puppy is about $5\frac{1}{2}$ inches long. The mother beagle is $3\frac{7}{11}$ times as long as the baby. How long is the mother?

34. Find the quotient. Write your answer in simplest form.
$\frac{1}{4} \div \frac{15}{16}$

35. A standard 2-by-4 board is 8 feet long. How many $1\frac{1}{4}$-foot stakes can you make out of one standard 2-by-4? How much wood will you have left over?

36. Solve. $\frac{9}{5}d = 1\frac{4}{5}$

37. The city bus stops in front of your house every half hour from 6:00 A.M. to 8:00 P.M. How many times does the bus stop in front of your house in a week?

38. What unit of measurement would you most likely use to measure the length of a football field?

39. Complete the statement.
216 in. = __?__ yd

40. Make a line plot of the following
test scores:
80, 85, 90, 95, 100, 85, 90, 85, 95

41. Find the range for the data set in
Exercise 40.

42. Find the mode for the data set in
Exercise 40.

43. Which type of data display, a bar graph or
a line graph, is more appropriate for
displaying the following data? Explain.

Sales at a golf shop:

January: $35,000

February: $25,000

March: $28,000

April: $36,000

**Use the following spreadsheet for
Exercises 44 and 45.**

	A	B	C	D
1	Date	Instrument Sales ($)	Music Sales ($)	Total Sales ($)
2	10-22-06	866	241	
3	10-23-06	1,243	259	

44. What is the value in cell C2?

45. Write the formula for cell D3.

46. Which measurement, the mean or the
median, more accurately describes the data
in the following data display?

2 | 99
3 | 01 12 15 18
5 | 66 79

Key: 2 | 99 means 299.

Mid-Course Test

Form D

Chapters 1–6

1. Write ten and forty-six thousandths in standard form.

2. Order the decimals from least to greatest.
   4.3, 4.19, 4.299, 4.2, 3.99

3. Round 67.32 to the tens place.

4. Find the sum. $1.46 + 9.3 + 0.7$

5. Explain how you would use mental math to divide 7.6 by 100.

6. Evaluate the expression.
   $12.1 \div (11 \times 11) + 0.9$

7. Write a rule to describe the number pattern.
   $5, 15, 45, 135, \ldots$

8. Evaluate the expression for the given values.
   $3x - 7y$ for $x = 12$ and $y = 3$

9. Solve. $x + 1.6 = 3$

10. Solve. $12x = 30$.

11. Write $2 \times 2 \times 2 \times p \times p \times p \times p \times p$ using exponents.

12. Evaluate. $(3^2 - 8)^2 + 5^2$

13. Rewrite $4(f + 3)$ using the Distributive Property.

14. What kind of numbers are NOT divisible by two?

15. The prime factorization of a number is $2 \times 2 \times 3 \times 5 \times 5$. What is the number?

16. The GCF of 28 and some other number is 7. What are the two least possible values for the other number?

17. What fraction is plotted on the number line?

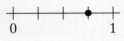

18. Write an improper fraction with a denominator of 12 that is equivalent to two and one fourth.

19. The prime factorizations of two numbers are $2 \times 2 \times 2 \times 3 \times 7$ and $2 \times 2 \times 3 \times 5$. What is the LCM of the two numbers?

20. Tom ran $3\frac{1}{5}$ miles. John ran $3\frac{3}{20}$ miles. Who ran farther?

21. Write 0.45 as a fraction in simplest terms.

22. Round $22\frac{3}{8}$ in. to the nearest half inch.

23. $\frac{11}{23}$ of your class are girls. What fraction of the class is boys?

Mid-Course Test (continued)

Form D

Chapters 1–6

24. Write the difference in simplest form.

$\frac{2}{3} - \frac{1}{12}$

25. Write the sum in simplest form.

$11\frac{13}{14} + 3\frac{1}{7}$

26. Write the difference in simplest form.

$25\frac{1}{10} - 12\frac{4}{5}$

27. Solve. Write your answer in simplest form.

$15\frac{1}{3} = n + 4\frac{5}{6}$

28. You are going on a trip by plane. Your first flight arrives at 11:20 A.M. Your connection flight departs at 1:10 P.M. How long do you have to wait at the airport between flights?

29. A newborn kitten is about $3\frac{1}{2}$ inches long. The mother cat is 4 times as long as the baby. How long is the mother?

30. Find the quotient. Write your answer in simplest form.

$\frac{1}{2} \div \frac{11}{12}$

31. Solve. $\frac{7}{3}b = 2\frac{1}{3}$

32. A grandfather clock chimes every $\frac{1}{4}$ of an hour. How many times does it chime in a week?

33. What unit of measurement would you most likely use to measure the weight of a car?

Mid-Course Test (continued)

Form D

Chapters 1–6

34. Complete the statement.
504 h = ___?___ weeks

35. Make a line plot of the following test scores:
84, 88, 90, 94, 100, 88, 90, 90, 94

36. Find the range for the data set in Exercise 35.

37. Find the mode for the data set in Exercise 35.

38. Which type of data display, a bar graph or a line graph, is more appropriate for displaying the following data? Explain.

Sales at a gift shop:

January: $20,000

February: $16,000

March: $15,000

April: $16,500

Use the following spreadsheet for Exercises 39 and 40.

	A	B	C	D
1	Date	Book Sales ($)	Music Sales ($)	Total Sales ($)
2	11-02-06	554	683	
3	11-03-06	679	650	

39. What is the value in cell C2?

40. Write the formula for cell D3.

41. Which measurement, the mean or the median, more accurately describes the data in the following data display?

```
1 | 94
2 | 26 30 31 32
3 | 68 69
```

Key: 1 | 94 means 194.

Mid-Course Test

Chapters 1–6

Form E

1. Write one hundred, six and eight hundredths in standard form.

8. Evaluate the expression for the given values.
$9m + n$ for $m = 4$ and $n = 15$

2. Order the decimals from least to greatest.
6.09, 6.6, 6.2, 6.1, 6.59

9. Solve. $3.1 - x = 2$

3. Round 124.83 to the ones place.

10. Solve. $p \div 4 = 0.8$

4. Find the difference. $29.8 - 6.38$

5. Explain how you would use mental math to multiply 32.6 by 100.

11. Write $3 \times 3 \times 3 \times 3 \times k \times k$ using exponents.

6. Evaluate the expression.
$2.5 \div (5 \times 5) + 2.9$

12. Evaluate. $4^2 - (5^2 - 23)$

7. Write a rule to describe the number pattern.
10, 30, 50, 70, . . .

13. Rewrite $(7 + m) \cdot 3$ using the Distributive Property.

14. How do you know when a number is divisible by five?

15. The prime factorization of a number is $2 \times 3 \times 3 \times 3 \times 7$. What is the number?

16. The GCF of 36 and some other number is 9. What are the two least possible values for the other number?

17. What fraction is plotted on the number line?

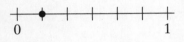

0   1

18. Write an improper fraction with a denominator of 6 that is equivalent to three and one half.

19. The prime factorizations of two numbers are $2 \times 3 \times 7$ and $2 \times 2 \times 3 \times 5$. What is the LCM of the two numbers?

20. Sally ran $2\frac{4}{5}$ miles. John ran $2\frac{6}{7}$ miles. Who ran farther?

21. Write 0.32 as a fraction in simplest terms.

22. Round $17\frac{3}{16}$ in. to the nearest half inch.

23. $\frac{7}{25}$ of your class are in the school play. What fraction of the class is not in the play?

Mid-Course Test (continued)

Form E

Chapters 1–6

24. Write the sum in simplest form.
$\frac{1}{2} + \frac{3}{16} + \frac{1}{8}$

25. Write the sum in simplest form.
$17\frac{11}{12} + 3\frac{2}{3}$

26. Write the difference in simplest form.
$18\frac{2}{15} - 9\frac{4}{5}$

27. Solve. Write your answer in simplest form.
$5\frac{1}{4} = n - \frac{7}{8}$

28. You are planning on going to two baseball games on Saturday. The first game is over at 2:50 P.M. The second game begins at 3:45 P.M. How long between games do you have to wait?

29. A newborn beagle puppy is about $5\frac{1}{2}$ inches long. The mother beagle is $3\frac{7}{11}$ times as long as the baby. How long is the mother?

30. Find the quotient. Write your answer in simplest form.
$\frac{1}{4} \div \frac{15}{16}$

31. Solve. $\frac{9}{5}d = 1\frac{4}{5}$

32. The city bus stops in front of your house every half hour from 6:00 A.M. to 8:00 P.M. How many times does the bus stop in front of your house in a week?

33. What unit of measurement would you most likely use to measure the length of a football field?

34. Complete the statement.
216 in. = __?__ yd

35. Make a line plot of the following test scores:
80, 85, 90, 95, 100, 85, 90, 85, 95

36. Find the range for the data set in Exercise 35.

37. Find the mode for the data set in Exercise 35.

38. Which type of data display, a bar graph or a line graph, is more appropriate for displaying the following data? Explain.

Sales at a golf shop:

January: $35,000

February: $25,000

March: $28,000

April: $36,000

Use the following spreadsheet for Exercises 39 and 40.

	A	B	C	D
1	Date	Instrument Sales ($)	Music Sales ($)	Total Sales ($)
2	10-22-06	866	241	
3	10-23-06	1,243	259	

39. What is the value in cell C2?

40. Write the formula for cell D3.

41. Which measurement, the mean or the median, more accurately describes the data in the following data display?

```
2 | 99
3 | 01 12 15 18
5 | 66 79
```

Key: 2 | 99 means 299.

Final Test
Chapters 1–12

Form A

1. What is the value of the digit 6 in 43.16?

2. Round 170.366 to the nearest hundredth.

3. Which property is represented by this mathematical statement?
$8 + 1 = 1 + 8$

4. Find the sum. $19.2 + 60.75 + 0.1$

5. Dan earns $6.90 per hour cutting grass. How much does he earn in 37.5 hours?

6. Evaluate the expression.
$8p - (2p + 5)$ for $p = 1.5$

7. Write a word phrase that describes the algebraic expression $12m + 3$.

8. Solve the equation. $k + 3.4 = 9$

9. If 6 times m is equal to 42, what is the value of m?

10. Find the missing exponent that makes the equation true.
$108 = 4 \times 3^{\underline{?}}$

11. Find all the digits that make $1,93\underline{?}$ divisible by both 2 and 3.

12. Which of the following numbers is NOT prime?
$7, 17, 27, 37$

13. Write $\frac{18}{22}$ in simplest form.

14. Compare. Fill in the $\underline{?}$ with $<, >,$ or $=$.
$2\frac{4}{9} \underline{\quad?\quad} \frac{7}{3}$

15. Write each fraction as a decimal. Then find the difference as a decimal.
$\frac{1}{4} - \frac{5}{25}$

16. Replace the __?__ with a number that will make the equation true.

$\frac{3}{11} + \frac{?}{11} = \frac{10}{11}$

17. Find the sum. Write your answer in simplest form.

$\frac{1}{9} + \frac{1}{18} + \frac{2}{3}$

18. At birth, one puppy weighs $\frac{15}{16}$ pounds. A second puppy weighs $1\frac{1}{8}$ pounds. How much more did the second puppy weigh?

19. Solve. $x + 3\frac{7}{9} = 7\frac{1}{3}$

20. A movie ends at 7:45 P.M. The next movie begins 50 minutes later. What time does the next movie begin?

21. Find the product. Write your answer in simplest form.

$\frac{10}{24} \cdot \frac{16}{18}$

22. Which quotient is NOT equal to the others?

$\frac{2}{3} \div \frac{1}{2}, \frac{2}{9} \div \frac{1}{6}, \frac{1}{2} \div \frac{3}{2}, \frac{4}{9} \div \frac{1}{3}$

23. Solve. $12\frac{1}{2}r = 2\frac{1}{2}$

24. Add.

$\begin{array}{r} 8 \text{ ft} \quad 7 \text{ in.} \\ + \ 9 \text{ ft} \ 11 \text{ in.} \\ \hline \end{array}$

25. Use $<, >,$ or $=$ to complete the statement.

100 oz __?__ $6\frac{1}{2}$ lb

26. Write the ratio 48 : 64 in simplest form.

27. It takes 3 cups of flour to make 24 cookies. How many cups of flour will you need to make 60 cookies?

28. Write 45% as a decimal and as a fraction in simplest form.

29. 85 out of 200 workers in a building arrive at 8:00 A.M. What percent of workers in the building do NOT arrive at 8:00 A.M.?

30. Write 750% as a decimal.

31. Find the mean, median, and mode of the data set to the nearest tenth.

4.5, 7, 4.1, 6.5, 7.1, 6.5, 5.3

© Pearson Education, Inc., publishing as Pearson Prentice Hall

Final Test (continued)

Form A

Chapters 1–12

Use the line graph below for Exercises 32–33.

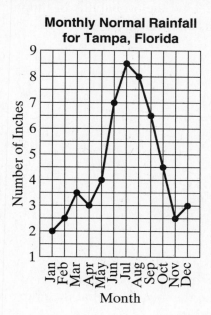

Monthly Normal Rainfall for Tampa, Florida

32. In which month is the amount of rainfall the greatest?

33. What is the range of the data?

Use the circle graph below for Exercises 34–35.

Origin of Zoo Animals

North America 30%
Africa 25%
Asia 12.5%
South America 20%
Australia 7.5%
Europe 5%

34. What percent of zoo animals did NOT originate in North America?

35. What percent of zoo animals originated in North or South America?

Use the diagram below for Exercises 36–37.

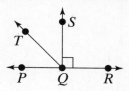

36. Name two complementary angles.

37. Name an obtuse angle.

38. △*DEF* is congruent to △*UVW*. The length of side *DE* is 6 cm , *EF* is 7.5 cm, and *DF* is 5 cm. What is the length of side *VW*?

39. True or False: When you rotate a figure about a point, its size remains the same.

40. Convert 420,000 mL to L.

41. The perimeter of a rectangle is 64 feet. If one side of the rectangle has a length of 20 feet, how long is the other side?

42. Find the area of the figure to the right.

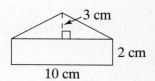

43. Find the circumference and the area of a circle with diameter equal to 8.6 inches. Use 3.14 for π.

44. A rectangular prism measures 8 m by 4 m by 5 m. What is its volume?

45. Write an integer to represent 400 feet below sea level.

46. Solve. $(-1) + (-2)$

47. The product or quotient of two negative numbers results in what kind of number?

48. Is the point $(4, -6)$ on the graph of $y = x - 10$?

49. If you roll a number cube, what is the probability that you will roll a number greater than four?

50. A hat contains slips of paper with the letters A–Z printed on them. If you draw one at random, what is the probability that you will get a vowel?

51. The probability that it will rain on a given day during the rainy season in Miami is 70%. If there are 140 days in the rainy season, on how many days should you expect it to rain?

52. You flip a coin twice, then roll a number cube. Find the probability of flipping two heads and rolling a 6.

53. Solve. $4m - 7 = 13$

54. Solve. $14 + \frac{k}{3} = 17$

55. Write the inequality that the graph below represents.

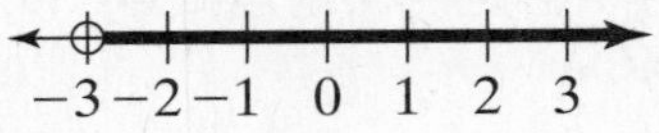

56. Solve. $12 + d > 112$

57. Triangle ABC is a right triangle. Find the missing side length.
$a = 12, b = ?, c = 15$

58. A triangle has sides of length 9, 12 and 14 cm. Is the triangle a right triangle?

Final Test

Chapters 1–12

1. What is the value of the digit 2 in 193.24?

2. Round 49.52 to the nearest tenth.

3. Which property is represented by this mathematical statement?
   $(3 + 2) + 1 = 3 + (2 + 1)$

4. Find the sum. $12.8 + 10.24 + 8.06$

5. Mary earns $5.25 per hour babysitting. How much does she earn in 20 hours?

6. Evaluate the expression.
   $6x + (4x - 7)$ for $x = 2.5$

7. Write a word phrase that describes the algebraic expression $\frac{k}{3} - 7$.

8. Solve the equation. $p - 1.6 = 7.2$

9. If c divided by 18 is equal to 4, what is the value of c?

10. Find the missing base that makes the equation true.
    $\underline{\ ?\ }^3 - 25 = 100$

11. Find all the digits that make 6,04$\underline{\ ?\ }$ divisible by both 2 and 3.

12. Which of the following numbers is NOT prime?
    3, 13, 23, 33

13. Write $\frac{39}{45}$ in simplest form.

14. Compare. Fill in the $\underline{\ ?\ }$ with $<, >,$ or $=$.
    $7\frac{1}{5} \underline{\ ?\ } \frac{72}{10}$

15. Write each fraction as a decimal. Then find the difference as a decimal.
    $\frac{9}{20} - \frac{1}{5}$

16. Replace the __?__ with a number that will make the equation true.
$\frac{2}{19} + \frac{?}{19} = \frac{15}{19}$

17. Find the difference. Write your answer in simplest form.
$\frac{17}{20} - \frac{1}{10} - \frac{1}{4}$

18. At birth, one kitten weighs $9\frac{1}{2}$ ounces. A second kitten weighs $10\frac{1}{4}$ ounces. How much more did the second kitten weigh?

19. Solve. $x - 6\frac{7}{8} = 1\frac{1}{4}$

20. A movie ends at 6:20 P.M. The next movie begins 50 minutes later. What time does the next movie begin?

21. Find the product. Write your answer in simplest form.
$\frac{45}{50} \cdot \frac{12}{15}$

22. Which quotient is NOT equal to the others?
$\frac{3}{7} \div \frac{1}{2}, \frac{2}{3} \div \frac{4}{7}, \frac{7}{3} \div \frac{2}{1}, \frac{7}{8} \div \frac{3}{4}$

23. Solve. $9\frac{2}{3}z = 5\frac{4}{5}$

24. Subtract.
   8 ft 7 in.
 $-$ 3 ft 9 in.

25. Use $<, >,$ or $=$ to complete the statement.
$3\frac{1}{2}$ ft __?__ 40 in.

26. Write the ratio 63 : 72 in simplest form.

27. Five pencils cost $0.75. How much will twelve pencils cost?

28. Write 65% as a decimal and as a fraction in simplest form.

29. 27 out of 60 people in a room are wearing either glasses or contact lenses. What percent of the people in the room are NOT wearing glasses or contact lenses?

30. Write 450% as a decimal.

31. Find the mean, median and mode of the data set.
9.2, 7.5, 8, 12.1, 8.4, 7.5, 10.3

Final Test (continued)

Chapters 1–12

Form B

Use the line graph below for Exercises 32–33.

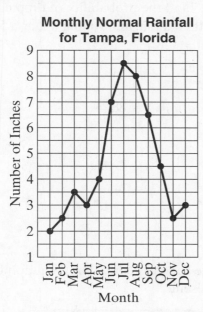

**Monthly Normal Rainfall
for Tampa, Florida**

32. In which month is the amount of rainfall the least?

33. How many inches did it rain in June, July, and August?

Use the circle graph below for Exercises 34–35.

Origin of Zoo Animals

North America 30%
Africa 25%
Asia 12.5%
South America 20%
Australia 7.5%
Europe 5%

34. What percent of zoo animals did NOT originate in Africa?

35. What percent of zoo animals originated in Asia, Australia, or Europe?

Use the diagram below for Exercises 36–37.

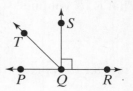

36. Name two supplementary angles.

37. Name an acute angle.

38. △*BCD* is congruent to △*HIJ*. The measure of ∠*D* is 50°, ∠B is 88°, and ∠*C* is 42°. What is the measure of ∠*I* ?

39. True or False: When you reflect a figure over a given line, the size of the figure changes.

40. Convert 5.3 km to m.

41. The area of a rectangle is 9.9 m². If one side of the rectangle has a length of 2.2 m, how long is the other side?

42. Find the area of the figure to the right.

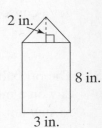

2 in.
8 in.
3 in.

43. Find the circumference and the area of a circle with a radius equal to 4.2 cm. Use 3.14 for π.

44. A rectangular prism measures 12 ft by 2 ft by 7 ft. What is its volume?

45. Write an integer to represent 35°F below zero.

46. Solve. $(-3) + (-4)$

47. The product of five negative numbers results in what kind of number?

48. Is the point $(-5, 3)$ on the graph of $y = x - 8$?

49. If you roll a number cube, what is the probability that you will roll a number less than four?

50. A hat contains slips of paper with the letters A–Z printed on them. If you draw one at random, what is the probability that you will get a consonant?

51. The probability that it will snow on a given day on a mountain top is 80%. If you plan to stay ten days on top of a mountain, on how many days should you expect it to snow?

52. You flip a coin twice, then roll a number cube. Find the probability of flipping a head and then a tail, and rolling a 3 or a 5.

53. Solve. $9n + 7 = 88$

54. Solve. $21 + \frac{r}{7} = 24$

55. Write the inequality that the graph below represents.

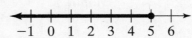

56. Solve. $15 + p \le 69$

57. Triangle ABC is a right triangle. Find the missing side length. $a = 16, b = ?, c = 20$

58. A triangle has sides of length 8, 12, and 15 cm. Is the triangle a right triangle?

Final Test

Form D

Chapters 1–12

1. What is the value of the digit 6 in 43.16?

2. Round 170.366 to the nearest hundredth.

3. Which property is represented by this mathematical statement?
   $8 + 1 = 1 + 8$

4. Find the sum. $19.2 + 60.75 + 0.1$

5. Dan earns \$6.90 per hour cutting grass. How much does he earn in 37.5 hours?

6. Evaluate the expression.
   $8p - (2p + 5)$ for $p = 1.5$

7. Solve the equation. $k + 3.4 = 9$

8. If 6 times m is equal to 42, what is the value of m?

9. Find the missing exponent that makes the equation true.
   $108 = 4 \times 3 \underline{}^{?}$

10. Find all the digits that make $1{,}93\underline{}$ divisible by 2.

11. Which of the following numbers is NOT prime?
    $7, 17, 27, 37$

12. Compare. Fill in the $\underline{}$ with $<, >$, or $=$.
    $2\frac{4}{9} \underline{} \frac{7}{3}$

13. Write each fraction as a decimal. Then find the difference as a decimal.
    $\frac{1}{4} - \frac{5}{25}$

14. Find the sum. Write your answer in simplest form.
    $\frac{1}{9} + \frac{1}{18} + \frac{2}{3}$

15. At birth, one puppy weighs $\frac{15}{16}$ pounds. A second puppy weighs $1\frac{1}{8}$ pounds. How much more did the second puppy weigh?

16. A movie ends at 7:45 P.M. The next movie begins 50 minutes later. What time does the next movie begin?

17. Find the product. Write your answer in simplest form.
$$\frac{10}{24} \cdot \frac{16}{18}$$

18. Which quotient is NOT equal to the others?
$$\frac{2}{3} \div \frac{1}{2}, \frac{2}{9} \div \frac{1}{6}, \frac{1}{2} \div \frac{3}{2}, \frac{4}{9} \div \frac{1}{3}$$

19. Solve. $12\frac{1}{2}\,r = 2\frac{1}{2}$

20. Add.
$$\begin{array}{r} 8 \text{ ft} \quad 7 \text{ in.} \\ + \ 9 \text{ ft} \ 11 \text{ in.} \\ \hline \end{array}$$

21. Use $<, >$, or $=$ to complete the statement.
100 oz ___?___ $6\frac{1}{2}$ lb

22. Write the ratio 48 : 64 in simplest form.

23. It takes 3 cups of flour to make 24 cookies. How many cups of flour will you need to make 60 cookies?

24. Write 45% as a decimal and as a fraction in simplest form.

25. 85 out of 200 workers in a building arrive at 8:00 A.M. What percent of workers in the building do NOT arrive at 8:00 A.M.?

26. Write 750% as a decimal.

27. Find the mean of the data set to the nearest tenth.
4.5, 7, 4.1, 6.5, 7.1, 6.5, 5.3

Final Test (continued)

Form D

Chapters 1–12

Use the line graph below for Exercises 28–29.

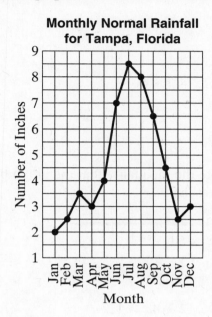

Monthly Normal Rainfall for Tampa, Florida

28. In which month is the amount of rainfall the greatest?

29. What is the range of the data?

Use the circle graph below for Exercises 30–31.

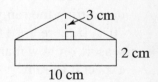

Origin of Zoo Animals

North America 30%
Africa 25%
Asia 12.5%
South America 20%
Australia 7.5%
Europe 5%

30. What percent of zoo animals did NOT originate in North America?

31. What percent of zoo animals originated in North or South America?

Use the diagram below for Exercises 32–33.

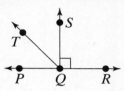

32. Name two complementary angles.

33. Name an obtuse angle.

34. $\triangle DEF$ is congruent to $\triangle UVW$. The length of side DE is 6 cm , EF is 7.5 cm, and DF is 5 cm. What is the length of side VW?

35. True or False: When you rotate a figure about a point, its size remains the same.

36. Convert 420,000 mL to L.

37. The perimeter of a rectangle is 64 feet. If one side of the rectangle has a length of 20 feet, how long is the other side?

38. Find the area of the figure to the right.

3 cm
2 cm
10 cm

39. Find the circumference and the area of a circle with diameter equal to 10 inches. Use 3.14 for π.

40. A rectangular prism measures 8 m by 4 m by 5 m. What is its volume?

41. Write an integer to represent 400 feet below sea level.

48. Solve. $4m - 7 = 13$

42. Solve. $(-1) + (-2)$

49. Solve. $14 + \frac{k}{3} = 17$

43. The product or quotient of two negative numbers results in what kind of number?

50. Write the inequality that the graph below represents.

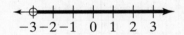

44. Is the point $(4, -6)$ on the graph of $y = x - 10$?

51. Solve. $12 + 4d > 112$

45. If you roll a number cube, what is the probability that you will roll a number greater than four?

52. Triangle ABC is a right triangle. Find the missing side length.
$a = 3, b = ?, c = 5$

46. The probability that it will rain on a given day during the rainy season in Miami is 70%. If there are 140 days in the rainy season, on how many days should you expect it to rain?

47. You flip a coin twice, then roll a number cube. Find the probability of flipping two heads and rolling a 6.

Final Test

Form E

Chapters 1–12

1. What is the value of the digit 2 in 193.24?

2. Round 49.52 to the nearest tenth.

3. Which property is represented by this mathematical statement?
   $(3 + 2) + 1 = 3 + (2 + 1)$

4. Find the sum. $12.8 + 10.24 + 8.06$

5. Mary earns $5.25 per hour babysitting. How much does she earn in 20 hours?

6. Evaluate the expression.
   $6x + (4x - 7)$ for $x = 2.5$

7. Solve the equation. $p - 1.6 = 7.2$

8. If c divided by 9 is equal to 4, what is the value of c?

9. Find the missing base that makes the equation true.
   $\underline{\ ?\ }^3 - 2 = 25$

10. Find all the digits that make 6,04$\underline{\ ?\ }$ divisible by 3.

11. Which of the following numbers is NOT prime?
    3, 13, 23, 33

12. Compare. Fill in the $\underline{\ ?\ }$ with $<$, $>$, or $=$.
    $7\frac{1}{5} \underline{\ ?\ } \frac{72}{10}$

13. Write each fraction as a decimal. Then find the difference as a decimal.
    $\frac{9}{20} - \frac{1}{5}$

14. Find the difference. Write your answer in simplest form.
$$\frac{17}{20} - \frac{1}{10} - \frac{1}{4}$$

15. At birth, one kitten weighs $9\frac{1}{2}$ ounces. A second kitten weighs $10\frac{1}{4}$ ounces. How much do the kittens weigh together?

16. A movie ends at 6:20 P.M. The next movie begins 50 minutes later. What time does the next movie begin?

17. Find the product. Write your answer in simplest form.
$$\frac{45}{50} \cdot \frac{12}{15}$$

18. Which quotient is NOT equal to the others?
$$\frac{3}{7} \div \frac{1}{2}, \frac{2}{3} \div \frac{4}{7}, \frac{7}{3} \div \frac{2}{1}, \frac{7}{8} \div \frac{3}{4}$$

19. Solve. $9\frac{2}{3}z = 5\frac{4}{5}$

20. Subtract.
$$\begin{array}{r} 8 \text{ ft } 7 \text{ in.} \\ - 3 \text{ ft } 9 \text{ in.} \\ \hline \end{array}$$

21. Use $<$, $>$, or $=$ to complete the statement.
$3\frac{1}{2}$ ft __?__ 40 in.

22. Write the ratio 63 : 72 in simplest form.

23. Five pencils cost $0.75. How much will twelve pencils cost?

24. Write 65% as a decimal and as a fraction in simplest form.

25. 27 out of 60 people in a room are wearing either glasses or contact lenses. What percent of the people in the room are NOT wearing glasses or contact lenses?

26. Write 450% as a decimal.

27. Find the median of the data set.
9.2, 7.5, 8, 12.1, 8.4, 7.5, 10.3

Final Test (continued)

Form E

Chapters 1–12

Use the line graph below for Exercises 28–29.

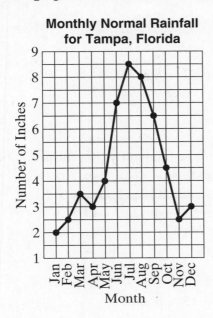

Monthly Normal Rainfall for Tampa, Florida

28. In which month is the amount of rainfall the least?

29. How many inches did it rain in June, July, and August?

Use the circle graph below for Exercises 30–31.

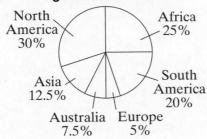

Origin of Zoo Animals

North America 30%
Africa 25%
South America 20%
Europe 5%
Australia 7.5%
Asia 12.5%

30. What percent of zoo animals did NOT originate in Africa?

31. What percent of zoo animals originated in Asia, Australia, or Europe?

Use the diagram below for Exercises 32–33.

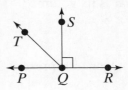

32. Name two supplementary angles.

33. Name an acute angle.

34. $\triangle BCD$ is congruent to $\triangle HIJ$. The measure of $\angle D$ is 50°, $\angle B$ is 88°, and $\angle C$ is 42°. What is the measure of $\angle I$?

35. True or False: When you reflect a figure over a given line, the size of the figure changes.

36. Convert 5.3 km to m.

37. The area of a rectangle is 9.9 m². If one side of the rectangle has a length of 2.2 m, how long is the other side?

38. Find the area of the figure to the right.

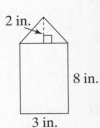

2 in.
8 in.
3 in.

39. Find the circumference and the area of a circle with a radius equal to 5 cm. Use 3.14 for π.

40. A rectangular prism measures 12 ft by 2 ft by 7 ft. What is its volume?

41. Write an integer to represent 35°F below zero.

42. Solve. $(-3) + (-4)$

43. The product of five negative numbers results in what kind of number?

44. Is the point $(-5, 3)$ on the graph of $y = x - 8$?

45. If you roll a number cube, what is the probability that you will roll a number less than four?

46. The probability that it will snow on a given day on a mountain top is 80%. If you plan to stay ten days on top of a mountain, on how many days should you expect it to snow?

47. You flip a coin twice, then roll a number cube. Find the probability of flipping a head and then a tail, and rolling a 3 or a 5.

48. Solve. $9n + 7 = 88$

49. Solve. $21 + \frac{r}{7} = 24$

50. Write the inequality that the graph below represents.

51. Solve. $15 + p \le 69$

52. Triangle ABC is a right triangle. Find the missing side length.
$a = 8, b = ?, c = 10$

Writing Gridded Responses
Exercises

Mark your answers on the grid for each exercise.

1. $5.32 + 4$

2. $4.8 \div 0.12$

3. 1.5×20

4. $17.3 - 14.88$

5. $6.5 - (4.1 + 0.6)$

6. You have $440 in a bank. You add $4 per week to the bank for the next six weeks. What is your balance at the end of six weeks?

Answering the Question Asked

Exercises

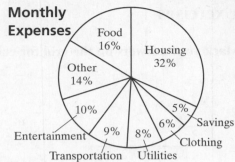

Monthly Expenses

Food 16%
Housing 32%
Other 14%
10% Entertainment
9% Transportation
8% Utilities
6% Clothing
5% Savings

Solve by answering the question asked.

1. A family's monthly expenses are summarized in the circle graph at the right.

   a. What percent of their income does the family spend on food *and* housing? Explain.

   A. 16%　　**B.** 32%　　**C.** 48%　　**D.** 50%

   _____

   _____

   _____

   b. What percent of their income does the family save?

   F. 5%　　**G.** 6%　　**H.** 8%　　**J.** 9%

   c. What percent of their income does the family *not* spend on food, clothing or housing?

   A. 16%　　**B.** 48%　　**C.** 54%　　**D.** 46%

2. The table at the right shows the number of boys participating in various sports at a high school.

Sport	Boys Participating
Baseball	21
Basketball	34
Football	62
Track	16
Wrestling	14

   a. How many boys participated in a sport other than football? Explain.

   F. 62　　**G.** 21　　**H.** 34　　**J.** 85

   _____

   _____

   _____

   _____

   b. How many boys participated in basketball *or* football?

   A. 34　　**B.** 96　　**C.** 62　　**D.** 86

Writing Short Responses

Exercises

Use the rubric below to answer each question.

Scoring Rubric

2 The variable is defined, the equation and the method used to solve it are correct, and the correct units are indicated. The solution is correct.

1 The variable is not defined, and there is no equation. However, there is a method to show how the problem was solved and the correct units are indicated.

1 A variable is defined, and an equation is written and solved. The response may contain minor errors.

0 There is no response, it is completely incorrect, or it is the correct response but there is no procedure shown.

1. The price of a skateboard is $74.95 plus tax. The total cost is $79.82. Define a variable. Write and solve an equation to find the amount of tax on the skateboard.

   Three responses are below with the points each received.

2 points	1 point	1 point
Let t = amount of tax. $74.95 + t = 79.82$ $74.95 + t = 79.82$ $-74.95 \quad -74.95$ $t = \;\; 4.87$ The amount of the tax is $4.87.	$79.82 - 74.95 = 4.87$ $4.87	Let t = amount of tax. $74.95 + t = 79.82$ $74.95 + t = 79.82$ $-74.95 \quad -74.95$ $t = \;\; 5.87$

   a. Explain why the second response received only 1 point.

   _____

   b. Explain why the third response received only 1 point.

   _____

   c. Write a different equation that could have been used to solve this problem.

   _____

   d. What type of answers might receive zero points?

   _____

2. The price of a model car is $16.45 plus the cost of the glue. The total cost is $17.50. Define a variable. Write and solve an equation to find the cost of the glue. Explain why the following response only received 1 point.
   "Let g = the cost of the glue. $16.45 + g = 17.50; g = \$1.25$"

   _____

Writing Extended Responses

Exercises

David has one quarter, three dimes, and five nickels. How many different ways can he combine the coins to make 45¢?

Scoring Rubric

- **4 points:** Student correctly answers question in a complete sentence, provides an explanation, and shows all possible combinations..

- **3 points:** Student answers question in a complete sentence, provides an explanation, and shows possible combinations, but makes minor calculation errors.

- **2 point:** Student provides an incorrect explanation and does not completely answer the question.

- **1 point:** Student incorrectly answers the question and does not provide an explanation.

- **0 points:** No response or answer is completely incorrect.

Three responses to the question are shown below.

4 point response	3 point response	1 point response
1 quarter, 2 dimes	1 quarter, 2 dimes	1 quarter, 2 dimes
1 quarter, 1 dime, 2 nickels	1 quarter, 1 dime, 2 nickels	
1 quarter, 4 nickels	1 quarter, 3 nickels	1 quarter, 1 dime, 2 nickels
3 dimes, 3 nickels	3 dimes, 3 nickels	
2 dimes, 5 nickels	2 dimes, 5 nickels	1 quarter, 4 nickels
There are no other possible ways for the coins to add up to 45¢ so this must be the complete answer.	These are the only combinations that add up to 45¢.	2 dimes, 5 nickels

1. Tell why the 4-point response received the points it did.

_____

_____

2. Read the 3-point response. What error did the student make?

_____

3. Write a 2-point response that has an incorrect explanation.

_____

_____

Reading for Understanding
Exercises

Use the passage that begins each exercise to answer the parts of the exercise.

1. Mr. Whitby's long-distance phone plan includes a $4.95 per month maintenance fee, $0.10 per minute for long-distance calls made from 6:00 A.M. to 6:00 P.M., and $0.05 per minute for long distance calls made after 6:00 P.M.

   In January, Mr. Whitby only made two long-distance calls. He made one of the calls at noon and the call lasted 17 minutes. He made the other call at 6:30 P.M. He finished this call at 6:53 P.M. How long did Mr. Whitby's second call last?

   a. What is the question asking for?

   _____

   b. Identify the information you need to solve the problem.

   _____

   c. How many minutes did Mr. Whitby's second call last?

   _____

   d. What was the cost of Mr. Whitby's first long-distance call in January?

   _____

   e. What was the cost of Mr. Whitby's second call?

   _____

   f. What was Mr. Whitby's total long-distance bill for January?

   _____

2. Mrs. Wilkinson has two apple trees and one pear tree in her backyard. Each apple tree produced $1\frac{3}{4}$ bushels of apples. The pear tree produced $2\frac{1}{3}$ bushels of pears.

   a. Which produced more per tree, the apple tree or the pear tree? How much more?

   _____

   b. How many total bushels of fruit did Mrs. Wilkinson's trees produce?

   _____

Eliminating Answers

Exercises

Identify the answer choices you can immediately eliminate. Cross the choices out and explain why you eliminated them. Then solve the problem.

1. Sandra is making 4 batches of cookies, so she will need to use 4 times the amount of flour the recipe calls for. The recipe calls for $3\frac{1}{4}$ cups of flour. How much flour does Sandra need?

   A. 12 cups   **B.** $1\frac{1}{4}$ cups   **C.** 13 cups   **D.** 17 cups

   _____

   _____

   _____

   _____

2. Alice's grandmother made a quilt that is $9\frac{1}{2}$ feet wide and $12\frac{5}{8}$ feet long. Alice plans to make a quilt that is half as wide and half as long. What will be the dimensions of Alice's quilt?

   F. $4\frac{3}{4}$ ft wide by $6\frac{5}{16}$ ft long   **G.** $4\frac{5}{8}$ ft wide by $6\frac{3}{8}$ ft long

   H. 4 ft wide by 6 ft long   **J.** $18\frac{1}{4}$ ft wide by $24\frac{1}{8}$ ft long

   _____

   _____

   _____

   _____

3. There are 95 different kinds of butterflies in a zoo. There are $\frac{4}{5}$ as many different kinds of beetles as butterflies at the zoo. How many different kinds of beetles are at the zoo?

   A. 76 beetles   **B.** 50 beetles   **C.** 120 beetles   **D.** 75 beetles

   _____

   _____

   _____

   _____

Working Backward
Exercises

Solve by working backward.

1. 72 is 40% of some number. Find the number.

   A. 28   **B.** 120   **C.** 180   **D.** 240

2. Solve the equation. $4x + 17 = 37$

   F. $x = 3$ **G.** $x = 5$ **H.** $x = 7$ **J.** $x = 10$

3. 75% of what number is 120?

   A. 110   **B.** 125   **C.** 145   **D.** 160

4. Solve the equation. $\frac{1}{2}x - 20 = 30$

   F. $x = 50$ **G.** $x = 100$ **H.** $x = 150$ **J.** $x = 200$

5. Adult tickets at the movie theater cost $7.50. Tickets for children under 12 years old cost $5.25. A group of people went to the movies and they paid a total of $97.50. How many of each type of ticket did the group buy?

   A. 8 adult tickets and 6 children tickets

   B. 6 adult tickets and 8 children tickets

   C. 6 adult tickets and 10 children tickets

   D. 4 adult tickets and 12 children tickets

6. Solve the equation. $4y + 60 = 100$

   F. 10   **G.** 20   **H.** 25   **J.** 40

7. 15% of 25 is what number?

   A. 21.25   **B.** 20   **C.** 15   **D.** 3.75

8. For what value of g is the equation true when $x = 10$?

   $\frac{g}{2}(x + 2) = 24$

   F. 2   **G.** 4   **H.** 6   **J.** 10

9. A flat of tulips costs $11.50. A flat of daffodils cost $15.25. A gardener paid $126 and purchased 6 flats of daffodils and a few flats of tulips. How many flats of tulips did the gardener purchase?

   A. 2 flats   **B.** 3 flats   **C.** 4 flats   **D.** 5 flats

Drawing a Picture

Exercises

Draw a diagram to solve each problem.

1. Point Q is the midpoint of $\overline{PR}$. $\overline{SQ}$ is perpendicular to $\overline{PR}$. Name two right angles. Explain.

   _____

   _____

   _____

2. An isosceles triangle is placed on top of a square. The base of the square is 6 cm and the base of the triangle is also 6 cm. The height of the triangle is 5 cm. What is the total area of the figure? Explain.

   _____

   _____

   _____

   _____

3. Point B is the vertex of angle ABC. The measure of angle ABC is 64°. Ray BD bisects angle ABC. What is the measure of angle ABD?

   _____

4. How many lines of symmetry can be drawn through an equilateral triangle?

   _____

5. How many lines of symmetry can be drawn through an isosceles triangle?

   _____

6. What are the only two quadrilaterals from which you can form 4 congruent triangles by drawing the diagonals?

   _____

Name _____ Class _____ Date _____

Measuring to Solve
••
Exercises

Use a protractor to answer each question.

1. Cathy's table is shaped like the trapezoid at the right.

   Find the measure of ∠Q to the nearest degree. _____

2. A quadrilateral is shown at the right.

   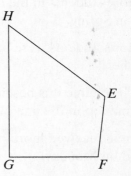

   Find the measure of ∠E to the nearest degree. _____

3. A brace for a shelf is shaped like the triangle at the right.

   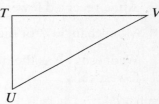

   Find the measure of ∠V to the nearest degree. _____

4. Coulter cuts the shape at the right out of paper.

   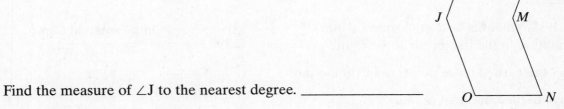

   Find the measure of ∠J to the nearest degree. _____

••

Interpreting Data

Exercises

Use the graphs at the right to answer each question.

1. Which statement is best supported by the information in the bar graph?

   A. Autumn birthdays were the most common.

   B. Winter birthdays were the least common.

   C. More students in the class were born in Autumn than in Spring.

   D. More students were born in Autumn than in Summer.

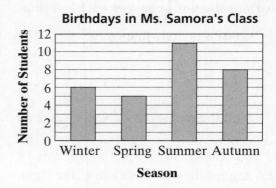

Birthdays in Ms. Samora's Class

2. Which statement is best supported by the information in the line plot at the right?

   F. Anne received more phone calls on Thursday than she did on Monday.

   G. Anne received fewer than 7 calls on Tuesday.

   H. More than 50% of the calls were received on Friday.

   J. Wednesday was the day on which Anne received the fewest calls.

Anne's Phone Calls

3. What was the mode of the data represented in the line plot?

   A. Monday

   B. Tuesday

   C. Thursday

   D. Friday

4. Which statement is best supported by the information in the bar graph at the right?

   F. George earned more points than Emilio did.

   G. Faye earned the least points.

   H. Two players earned the same number of points.

   J. Hina earned twice as many points as Iko.

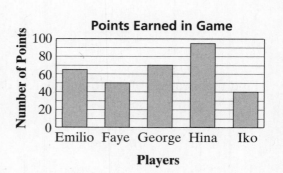

Points Earned in Game

Using a Variable

•••

Exercises

Define a variable. Then write and solve an equation for each problem.

1. Mr. Drake bought 84 horseshoes to shoe all of his horses. Each horse needs 4 shoes. How many horses does Mr. Drake have?

   _____

   _____

2. The price of a DVD is $17.99 plus tax. The total cost is $19.16. How much is the tax on the DVD?

   _____

   _____

3. Ed spends an average of $18 per week on gas. So far, he has spent a total of $216. How many weeks has he bought gas?

   _____

   _____

4. Troop 77 of the Girl Scouts made $342 by selling cookies. If each box of cookies costs $3, how many boxes did Troop 77 sell?

   _____

   _____

5. Maggie spent $30 at the county fair and all she did was go on the rides. If the cost of admission was $8 and each ride cost $2, how many rides did Maggie go on? Let r = the number of rides Maggie went on.

   a. Which equation below could be used to answer the question?

   A. $2r = 30$ **B.** $30 + 2r = 8$

   C. $8 + 2r = 30$ **D.** $8r + 2 = 30$

   b. Solve the equation in part (a) to find the number of rides Maggie rode.

   _____

Estimating the Answer

Exercises

Estimate each answer. Use 3 for π. Use estimation to eliminate choices.

1. The diameter of a cylindrical water barrel is 1.8 feet. The height of the barrel is 3.3 feet. Find the volume of the water barrel to the nearest tenth of a cubic foot. Explain your reasoning.

   A. 3.6 ft^3 **B.** 6.4 ft^3 **C.** 8.4 ft^3 **D.** 11.9 ft^3

   _____

   _____

   _____

   _____

2. Lisa is having a special dinner and needs to make tablecloths for 10 large round tables. She plans to add 2 feet to the diameter of the tables for the tablecloths, so they will drape over the edges. The diameter of each table is 7.8 feet. Lisa bought 500 square feet of material.

   a. Does she have enough to make all 10 tablecloths? Explain.

   _____

   _____

   _____

   _____

   _____

   _____

   b. If not, approximately how much more material will she need to buy?

   _____

3. The diameter of a round garden is 12 feet. To the nearest square foot, how much plastic would be required to cover the garden?

   F. 36 ft^2 **G.** 48 ft^2 **H.** 72 ft^2 **J.** 108 ft^2

4. To the nearest centimeter, find the circumference of a circle with a 5-centimeter radius.

   A. 15 cm   **B.** 24 cm   **C.** 30 cm   **D.** 75 cm

5. What is the approximate volume of a bucket that has a diameter of 10 inches and is 12 inches tall? _____

NAEP Practice Test

1. Alex had $280.79 in his savings account. Alex worked for Mrs. Gomez and earned $34.00 the first week and $52.93 the second week. Alex put all the money he earned into his savings account. What is the best estimate of how much money Alex had in his account after he worked for Mrs. Gomez?

   A $320.00

   B $340.00

   C $360.00

   D $380.00

   E $400.00

2. Between which two consecutive whole numbers does the $\sqrt{32}$ lie?

   A 2 and 3

   B 3 and 4

   C 4 and 5

   D 5 and 6

   E 6 and 7

3. Louise is making soup for a big family gathering. Her recipe for chicken soup calls for $\frac{2}{3}$ cup of chopped celery. The recipe makes enough soup for 4 people. How much celery would she need if she were making enough soup for 12 people?

   A $\frac{2}{3}$ cup

   B $\frac{4}{12}$ cup

   C 1 cup

   D $1\frac{2}{3}$ cups

   E 2 cups

4. To win a prize at the school carnival, students had to choose the jar with the most beans. The shaded part of each jar shows how full it was. Which jar was the fullest?

   A   **B**

   C   **D**

   E

GO ON

5. Which data set has the mode with the greatest value?

A 1, 4, 5, 6, 7, 5, 5, 7, 3, 5

B 4, 4, 5, 6, 7, 9, 12, 3, 1, 4

C 7, 3, 7, 9, 10, 15, 17, 3, 8, 3

D 2, 15, 18, 18, 18, 2, 3, 2, 3, 2

E 75, 80, 91, 23, 5, 4, 4, 17, 89, 30

6. Attendance for the first four performances of a school play was 104, 133, 128, and 71. Attendance for the last four performances was 122, 188, 162, and 112. How much more was the mean attendance of the last four performances than the mean attendance of the first four performances?

A 28

B 37

C 41

D 109

E 146

7. Barney's math textbook has 4 more chapters than the number of chapters, s, in his science textbook. Which expression represents the number of chapters in Barney's math textbook?

A s

B $s - 4$

C $4 \times s$

D $s + 4$

E $4 - s$

8. What is the value of the expression $5x + 12y$ if $x = 8$ and $y = 7$?

A 15

B 17

C 60

D 124

E 131

9. There are 286 students in the sixth grade at a certain middle school. Each row of chairs in the school auditorium seats 22 students. Which equation can be used to find the number of rows needed to seat all of the sixth grade students?

A $r = 22 \cdot 286$

B $\frac{r}{22} = 286$

C $r = \frac{286}{22}$

D $r = \frac{22}{286}$

E $\frac{r}{286} = 22$

10. If $x + 14 = 63$, then $x =$

A 4.5

B 21

C 49

D 77

E 882

GO ON

Name _____ Class _____ Date _____

11. Tim asked his brother to help him solve the equation $12 + a = 22$. His brother told Tim to solve the problem by adding 12 to both sides of the equation. What should Tim say to prove his brother wrong?

A No, I need to add 12 to just the right side of the equation.

B No, I need to add a to both sides of the equation.

C No, I need to subtract 22 from both sides of the equation

D No, I need to subtract 12 from both sides of the equation.

E No, I need to subtract a from both sides of the equation.

12. If $2x + 3 = 39$, then $x =$

A 13

B 18

C 19.5

D 21

E 42

13. Which equation represents the model?

A $6x = 16$

B $4x + 2 = 2x + 6$

C $4x - 2 = 2x - 6$

D $4x - 4 = 2x + 12$

E $4x + 4 = 2x + 12$

14. Which inequality represents the graph?

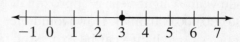

A $x \geq 3$

B $x < 3$

C $x \leq 3$

D $x > 3$

E $x \neq 3$

15. If $x - 4 < 12$, which number is **not** a solution?

A 8

B 10

C 12

D 14

E 16

16. If $x - 3 \leq 7$, then

A $x \leq 4$.

B $x \leq 10$.

C $x \geq 10$.

D $x < 4$.

E $x > 10$.

GO ON

17. A light-year is the distance that light travels in one year. A light-year is approximately 5,880,000,000,000 miles. How would the distance of one light-year be expressed in scientific notation?

A 5.88×10^9

B 58.8×10^{12}

C 5.88×10^{12}

D 5.8×10^{13}

E 1.00×10^{58}

18. Monroe is sorting his baseball cards into stacks of more than one card each. He has 133 cards. What is the greatest number of stacks Monroe can make if the stacks all have the same number of cards?

A 6

B 7

C 11

D 13

E 19

19. What is the prime factorization of 36?

A $2 \cdot 2 \cdot 2 \cdot 3$

B $2^2 \cdot 3^2$

C $2^2 \cdot 3^3$

D $3 \cdot 12$

E $1 \cdot 36$

20. Which fraction and decimal are equal to each other?

A $\frac{1}{8}$ and 0.125

B $\frac{1}{6}$ and 0.1667

C $\frac{1}{5}$ and 0.25

D $\frac{2}{3}$ and 0.66

E $\frac{3}{4}$ and 0.70

21. A carpenter cut $\frac{1}{2}$ inch off a board and discovered it was still too long. Then she cut off another $\frac{1}{3}$ inch. What was the total amount that the carpenter cut off the board?

A $\frac{1}{6}$ inch

B $\frac{1}{5}$ inch

C $\frac{2}{3}$ inch

D $\frac{5}{6}$ inch

E 1 inch

22. Roberto jogged from his house to a nearby park. Once there, he completed a jog on a trail. Then he jogged back home. The park is $1\frac{3}{4}$ miles from his house, and the trail is a loop $2\frac{2}{5}$ miles long. How many total miles did Roberto run?

A $4\frac{3}{20}$ miles

B $5\frac{3}{5}$ miles

C $5\frac{9}{10}$ miles

D $6\frac{1}{4}$ miles

E $8\frac{3}{10}$ miles

23. Find the product: $3\frac{2}{3} \times 2\frac{1}{4}$

A $4\frac{7}{12}$

B $5\frac{11}{12}$

C $6\frac{1}{6}$

D $6\frac{3}{7}$

E $8\frac{1}{4}$

24. Find the quotient: $2\frac{3}{5} \div 2\frac{1}{2}$

A $\frac{1}{10}$

B $1\frac{1}{25}$

C $4\frac{3}{10}$

D $5\frac{1}{10}$

E $6\frac{1}{2}$

25. Rhonda is measuring the distance around a flower garden in her backyard so that she can put bricks around its edge. Which unit of measurement should she use?

A centimeters

B inches

C feet

D miles

E kilometers

26. Josie kept track of the amount of gas she used while driving her car. The first week she used 12.8 gallons. The second week she used 14.37 gallons. The third week she used exactly 19 gallons. How many gallons of gas did Josie use altogether?

A 15.39 gallons

B 27.17 gallons

C 33.37 gallons

D 45.1 gallons

E 46.17 gallons

27. Which figure has the greatest ratio of *shaded area* to *non-shaded area*?

A
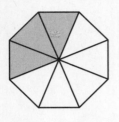

B
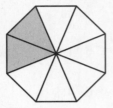

C
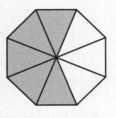

D
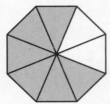

E
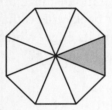

28. A car traveled 252 miles on the Interstate highway in 4 hours. If the car traveled at a steady speed, how many miles did the car travel in 1 hour?

A 52 miles

B 63 miles

C 65 miles

D 70 miles

E 1,008 miles

29. If you cross multiply to solve the proportion $\frac{x}{10} = \frac{6}{29}$, which equation could you use to solve the proportion?

A $29 = 6x$

B $10 = 29x$

C $(6)(29) = 10x$

D $(6)(10) = 29x$

E $10 = 6x$

30. If $\frac{10}{3} = \frac{x}{12}$, then $x =$

A 1.8.   **B** 5.

C 40.   **D** 80.

E 120.

31. Jamal is 6 feet tall, and his shadow is 4 feet long. At the same time of day, a tree near Jamal has a shadow that is 20 feet long. How tall is the tree?

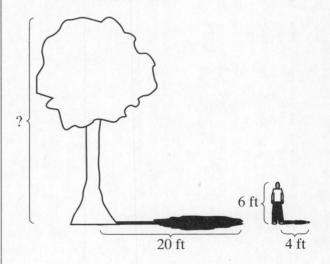

A 24 feet   **B** 30 feet

C 36 feet   **D** 60 feet

E 120 feet

32. Erika's grandfather builds small models of actual ships. He builds them to a scale of 1 inch = 3 feet. Based on the model shown below, what is the length of the actual ship?

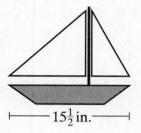

$\vdash\!\!-\,15\frac{1}{2}\,\text{in.}\,-\!\!\dashv$

A 3 feet

B $5\frac{1}{6}$ feet

C $15\frac{1}{2}$ feet

D 45 feet

E $46\frac{1}{2}$ feet

33. Carla's new computer printer can print 1,260 pages in 3 hours. At this rate, how many pages can it print in 1 minute?

A 7

B 10

C 21

D 105

E 420

34. Music Town had a sale on music CDs. If you bought 4 CDs, you got one free. Manuel bought 4 CDs for $12.99 each and got another CD valued at $12.99 for free. What was Manuel's percent of savings?

A 10%

B 12.9%

C 20%

D 25%

E 33%

35. There were 60 questions on Jessie's math test. He answered 15 incorrectly. What percent of the questions did Jessie answer correctly?

A 25%

B 36%

C 67%

D 75%

E 136%

36. About 480 students bring their own lunch to school. This number is 40% of the students at the school. About how many students attend the school?

A 720

B 1,200

C 1,920

D 2,880

E 3,200

37. Casey and her sister make beaded necklaces. The beads and other materials cost them $2.50 per necklace. Their selling price is 70% above their cost. How much do the sisters sell the necklaces for?

A $3.75

B $4.00

C $4.25

D $4.50

E $4.75

38. Which segment intersects $\overline{DE}$?

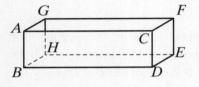

A $\overline{BH}$

B $\overline{CF}$

C $\overline{GH}$

D $\overline{BD}$

E $\overline{AG}$

39. What kind of triangle is shown?

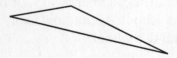

A acute triangle

B equilateral triangle

C isosceles triangle

D right triangle

E scalene triangle

40. What is the measure of $\angle R$ in the triangle?

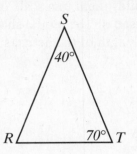

A 40°

B 60°

C 70°

D 72°

E 180°

41. What is the name of the figure shown?

A parallelogram

B trapezoid

C rhombus

D square

E rectangle

42. Which polygon is a rhombus?

A
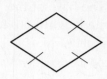

B

C
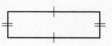

D

E
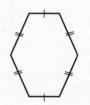

43. How many lines of symmetry does this figure have?

A 0

B 1

C 2

D 4

E 8

44. What is the sum of the angle measures for the figure?

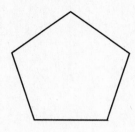

A 180°

B 360°

C 540°

D 720°

E 900°

45. Triangles ABC and RPQ are similar. What is the length of side QR?

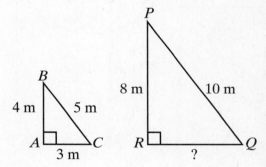

A 3 m

B 4 m

C 5 m

D 6 m

E 8 m

> GO ON

46. A circle has a diameter of 20 inches. What is the circle's radius?

   A 3.14 inches

   B 5 inches

   C 10 inches

   D 12 inches

   E 62.8 inches

47. Students did a survey and asked 200 students to choose their favorite healthy food. How many students chose carrots?

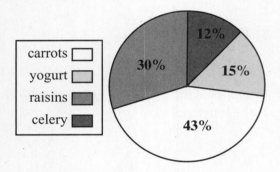

   A 43   **B** 60

   C 86   **D** 172

   E 200

48. What is the area of the figure?

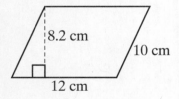

   A 120 cm^2 **B** 98.4 cm^2

   C 64 cm^2 **D** 44 cm^2

   E 20.2 cm^2

49. Maria is drawing a large triangle on a mural on the cafeteria wall. The base of the triangle is 7 feet and the height is 10 feet, what is the triangle's area?

   A 17.5 square feet

   B 24 square feet

   C 27 square feet

   D 35 square feet

   E 70 square feet

50. Volunteers are putting a new fence around a flower garden in a neighborhood park. How many feet of fence do the volunteers need to buy?

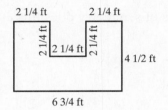

   A 27 ft

   B 29$\frac{1}{4}$ ft

   C 36 ft

   D 43$\frac{1}{2}$ ft

   E 54 ft

51. What is the circumference of the circle?

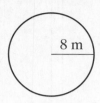

8 m

A 12.56 m   **B** 25.12 m

C 37.68 m   **D** 50.24 m

E 200.96 m

52. The rectangle is divided by two diagonals. How long is each diagonal?

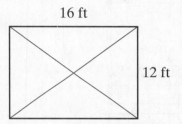

16 ft

12 ft

A 10 feet   **B** 18 feet

C 20 feet   **D** 28 feet

E 40 feet

53. Approximately how much cereal does this box hold?

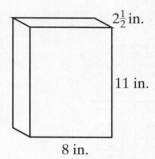

$2\frac{1}{2}$ in.

11 in.

8 in.

A 20 in.^{3} **B** $27\frac{1}{2}$ in.^{3}

C 88 in.^{3} **D** $115\frac{1}{2}$ in.^{3}

E 220 in.^{3}

54. If the pattern in the list below continues, what will be the next number?
10, 12, 11, 13, 12, 14, 13, . . .

A 12   **B** 14

C 15   **D** 17

E 18

55. Which rule tells how each term of the sequence, after the first, can be found from the one before it?
7, 12, 17, 22, 27, 32, . . .

A 12n

B $n + 5$

C $n - 5$

D $n \div 5$

E n^5

GO ON

56. Which function is represented on the graph?

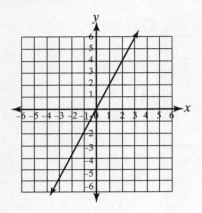

A $y = \frac{x}{2}$ **B** $y = 2x^2$

C $y = 2 + x$ **D** $y = -2x$

E $y = 2x$

57. Which of the following ordered pairs is NOT a solution to $y = x - 3$?

A $(1, 3)$ **B** $(2, -1)$

C $(3, 0)$ **D** $(7, 4)$

E $(15, 12)$

58. Which rule is shown by the following table?

x	y
0	0
1	0.5
3	1.5
8	4

A $y = 2x$ **B** $y = \frac{x}{2}$

C $y = x - 2$ **D** $y = x + 2$

E $y = \frac{x}{2} - 1$

59. Which is a graph of a linear function?

A

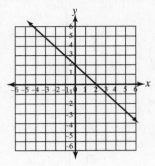

B

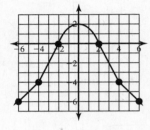

C

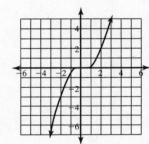

D

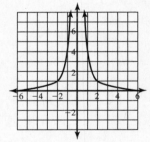

E

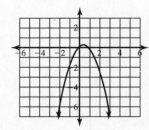

GO ON

60. What are the next two shapes in the pattern below?

□ ☆ □ △ □ ○ □ ☆

A □ ○　　　　　**B** □ ☆

C △ □　　　　　**D** □ △

E ○ □

61. A toy company makes remote-controlled cars. A worker randomly selects 200 cars to inspect. The sample has 3 faulty cars. If the company makes 10,000 cars a month, predict how many of the 10,000 cars will be faulty.

A 3　　　　　　　**B** 60

C 150　　　　　　**D** 200

E 600

62. A box contains 1 blue marble, 1 red marble, 1 yellow marble, and 1 green marble. You take a marble at random from the bag and put it back. You draw a second time and, again, put the marble back. Then you draw again. What is the probability that you will draw a yellow marble 3 times in a row?

A $\frac{1}{4}$　　　　　　**B** $\frac{1}{8}$

C $\frac{1}{16}$　　　　　**D** $\frac{1}{32}$

E $\frac{1}{64}$

63. Greg tossed a coin 100 times and got 36 heads and 64 tails. What is the difference between the theoretical probability and the experimental probability of tossing heads?

A $\frac{9}{25}$　　　　　　**B** $\frac{7}{50}$

C $\frac{64}{100}$　　　　　**D** $\frac{1}{2}$

E $\frac{8}{25}$

Short Constructed Response

64. Explain how you would find the 10th term of the following sequence: 3, 7, 11, 15, 19, ...

65. In science class, students were playing with spinning tops to see who could make their top spin the longest. Ali's top spun for 35 seconds. Maggie's top spun for 37 seconds. Dan's top spun for 38 seconds. Cori's top spun for 46 seconds. Make a chart, graph, or table that shows the results of the students' experiments.

66. Carlos is planting a tree and needs to support it with 3 wooden stakes. The bottom end of each stake will rest on the ground, 3 feet from the bottom of the tree. The top end of each stake will attach to the tree, 4 feet up from the ground. The tree forms a right angle with the ground. How many feet of wood are required for Carlos to complete his job? Justify your answer by including a diagram.

67. A rectangular-shaped playground is 20 yards wide and 35 yards long. The local playground association wants to put a wood fence around the playground along its edge. The fence comes in 8-foot-long sections.

How many sections of fence will be needed?

Can the playground be fenced without cutting any of the sections? Explain.

68. Over three days, the 8th grade class at a certain middle school voted on where they would go for their class trip. The graph below shows how many students chose each of the destinations. According to the graph, where should the class go on its trip? Explain.

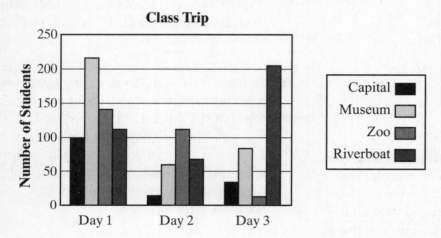

69. Roberta knows that $x < y$ and that $x > 0$ and $y > 0$. She claims that $x^2 < y^2$. Is she correct? Why or why not?

70. Annie likes to fly her airplane to see her Uncle Theo. She can take the scenic route from her town, flying 12 miles due north, then 9 miles due west. She can also take the shorter route, which goes directly from her town to Theo's town. If it costs $0.75 in fuel to fly 1 mile, how much money does Annie save by taking the shorter route? Justify your answer by including a diagram.

SAT 10 Practice Test

∙∙

PS *Mathematics: Problem Solving*

Read each question. Then mark your answer on the answer sheet.

1. **Which of the following shows these numbers in correct order from least to greatest?**

   A 0.4, 0.39, 0.06, 0.51

   B 0.06, 0.39, 0.4. 0.51

   C 0.06, 0.4, 0.39, 0.51

   D 0.4, 0.06, 0.39, 0.51

2. **Of the numbers $\frac{3}{7}$, $\frac{5}{9}$, $\frac{7}{10}$, and $\frac{3}{5}$, which is the greatest?**

   F $\frac{7}{10}$ **H** $\frac{5}{9}$

   G $\frac{3}{5}$ **J** $\frac{3}{7}$

3. **Which of the following does NOT describe 0.56?**

   A $56 \div 100$ **C** $\frac{56}{100}$

   B 56%   **D** 56:44

4. **Inez bought $\frac{7}{8}$ pound of mixed nuts. What is another way of expressing this number?**

   F 0.625   **H** 78%

   G 0.7   **J** 0.875

5. **Which of the following are equivalent fractions for $\frac{6}{18}$?**

   A $\frac{1}{3}$ and $\frac{3}{9}$ **C** $\frac{1}{4}$ and $\frac{3}{9}$

   B $\frac{1}{3}$ and $\frac{2}{9}$ **D** $\frac{1}{4}$ and $\frac{2}{8}$

6. **Pluto has an approximate distance of 3,573,240,000 miles from Earth. Which of the following shows this number written in words?**

   F Three million, five hundred seventy-three thousand, two hundred forty

   G Three million, five hundred seventy-three thousand, two hundred forty thousand

   H Three billion, five hundred seventy-three, two hundred forty

   J Three billion, five hundred seventy-three million, two hundred forty thousand

7. **The airport bus arrives at the bus station every 32 minutes. The city bus arrives at the bus station every 6 minutes. To find out how often both buses arrive at the bus station at the same time, find the least common multiple of 32 and 6.**

   A Every 36 minutes

   B Every 64 minutes

   C Every 96 minutes

   D Every 128 minutes

∙∙

8. **Which is the value of the 6 in 2,378,604,117?**

    F 6,000,000   **H** 60,000

    G 600,000   **J** 6,000

9. **Which is the place value of the 5 in 421.365?**

    A Thousandths   **C** Tenths

    B Hundredths   **D** Thousands

10. **According to the 1990 census, the population of Philadelphia was 5,899,345. If the 1991 census had increased by 1000 people, what would the 1991 population of Philadelphia have been?**

    F 5,800,345   **H** 6,100,345

    G 5,900,345   **J** 6,899,345

11. **Which of the following is equivalent to (2 × 1,000,000) + (5 × 100,000) + (4 × 10,000) + 1000?**

    A 2,541   **C** 2,541,000

    B 254,100   **D** 25,410,000

12. **Bill collects baseball cards. He gets 6 new cards every other day. Which of the following number sentences will help Bill figure out how many cards he will have saved at the end of 30 days?**

    F 6 × 15 = 90

    G 30 + 6 = 36

    H 6 × 30 = 180

    J 30 + 6 = 5

13. **Which expression Is NOT equivalent to 45?**

    A 0 + 45   **C** 45 + 0

    B 9 × 5   **D** 0 × 45

14. **Tim needs to buy computer disks. One box of 20 computer disks costs $7.95. About how much does one computer disk cost?**

    F $0.50   **H** $0.30

    G $0.40   **J** $0.20

15. **Find the next number in the pattern. 64, 54, 45, 37, 30, . . .**

    A 24   **C** 20

    B 22   **D** 18

16. **What is the next figure in the sequence of figures?**

F   **H**

G   **J**

GO ON

PS **SAT 10 Practice Test**

17. Use the function table to help you find the value of *y* when *x* = 5.

x	y
0	6
1	8
2	10
3	12

A 15   **C** 20

B 16   **D** 22

18. Max's Diner has three kinds of soup: chicken, vegetable, and tomato. The diner also has two kinds of bread: wheat and white. If a special consists of one choice of soup and one choice of bread, how many different specials are possible?

F 3 specials   **H** 9 specials

G 6 specials   **J** 12 specials

19. There are 14 red apples and 12 green apples in a bag. If an apple is chosen at random, what is the probability that it will be red?

A $\frac{6}{13}$ **C** $\frac{7}{13}$

B $\frac{1}{2}$ **D** $\frac{7}{6}$

20. Simplify the expression.
$2 + 2^3 \times 3 + 3$

F 33   **H** 27

G 29   **J** 16

21. At the end of a game, two players are tied. This spinner will be spun one time, and the number that comes up will determine the winner. Player A wins if the number is greater than 3; otherwise Player B wins. Which is the most likely outcome?

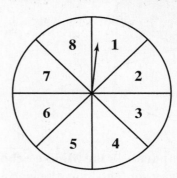

A Player B will win because there are more chances to land on a number greater than 3.

B There will be another tie with neither player winning.

C Player A will win because the tie-breaking game is not fair.

D Player B will win because the tie-beaking game is not fair.

22. The heights of five plants are 9 cm, 6 cm, 5 cm, 9 cm, and 8 cm. What is the median height in centimeters of these plants?

F 5 cm   **H** 8 cm

G 7.4 cm   **J** 9 cm

>**GO ON**

PS SAT 10 Practice Test

Use the circle graph below to answer Questions 23 and 24.

Middle School Band

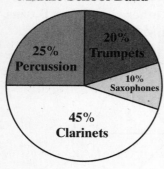

23. There are 60 students in the Middle School Band. How many students play the clarinet?

A 32 students   C 25 students

B 27 students   D 15 students

24. Which instrument seems to be the most popular with the students in the Middle School Band?

F Percussion   H Clarinet

G Saxophone   J Trumpet

25. The frequency table shows the number of pets per student in Mr. Perez's class. How many students have more than 2 pets?

Number of Pets	Number of Students
0	7
1	12
2	5
3	5
4 or more	2

A 5 students   C 11 students

B 7 students   D 12 students

26. This line graph shows outdoor temperature readings taken at one-hour intervals. According to the graph, what was the temperature reading at 9:30 A.M.?

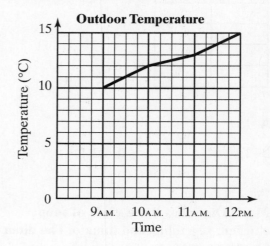

F 10°C   H 12°C

G 11°C   J 13°C

27. Laura rolled a number cube 30 times. She recorded the results in the tally chart below. How many times did she roll the number 5?

1	ⅢⅠ
2	Ⅱ
3	ⅢⅠ
4	ⅢⅠ
5	Ⅲ ⅢⅠ
6	Ⅲ

A 5 times   C 9 times

B 8 times   D 14 times

Name_____ Class_____ Date_____

PS SAT 10 Practice Test

28. Benjamin drew the following angle. How would you classify the angle?

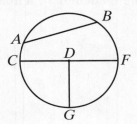

157°

F Straight   **H** Right

G Obtuse   **J** Acute

29. Which segment represents a radius of the circle with center *D*?

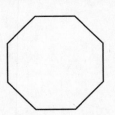

A *AB*   **C** *DG*

B *CF*   **D** *BA*

30. How many lines of symmetry does the figure below have?

F 4   **H** 8

G 6   **J** 12

31. What is the value of *n*? $n - 12 = 45$

  A 33   **C** 57

  B 48   **D** 60

32. Which number sentence goes with $37 + 5 = \square$?

F $37 \times 5 = \square$ **H** $\square - 5 = 37$

G $\square + 5 = 37$ **J** $5 \div \square = 37$

33. Use the diagram of May's garden to determine how many feet of fencing she will need to enclose the entire garden.

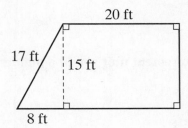

20 ft

17 ft   15 ft

8 ft

A 60 ft   **C** 80 ft

B 72 ft   **D** 95 ft

34. What are the coordinates of triangle *PQR*?

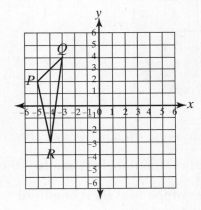

F $P(5, 3), Q(3, 4), R(4, -3)$

G $P(-5, 2), Q(-3, 4), R(-4, -3)$

H $P(-5, 2), Q(-3, -4), R(-4, 3)$

J $P(-5, -2), Q(-3, 4), R(4, -3)$

35. **What is the length of the pencil below? Use a metric ruler to find out. Round to the nearest centimeter.**

    A 7 cm

    B 13 cm

    C 14 cm

    D 22 cm

36. **Which measurement unit would a builder most likely use when measuring the length of a house?**

    F millimeters

    G centimeters

    H meters

    J kilometers

37. **Compare the area of the large shaded triangle to the area of the rectangle.**

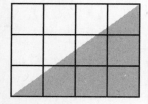

    A The area of the triangle is twice the area of the rectangle.

    B The area of the triangle is one-half the area of the rectangle.

    C The area of the triangle is one-third the area of the rectangle.

    D The area of the triangle is one-fourth the area of the rectangle.

38. **The bus leaves Bound Brook at 2:55 P.M. and arrives in Hillside at 4:20 P.M. How long does the bus ride last?**

    F 7 hr, 15 min   **H** 1 hr, 25 min

    G 1 hr, 65 min   **J** 1 hr, 15 min

PS SAT 10 Practice Test

39. **Mrs. Lee's class is made up of 29 students. Each student received 4 ounces of candy hearts on Valentine's Day. How many pounds of candy hearts did Mrs. Lee distribute to her students?**

    A 6 lb

    B 7 lb

    C $7\frac{1}{4}$ lb

    D 7.4 lb

40. **Rosalie is planning a bike trip. She wants to know how far it is from the parking lot to the lake. She found the map below.**

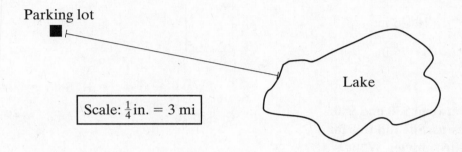

Parking lot

Lake

Scale: $\frac{1}{4}$ in. = 3 mi

    On the map, the distance from the parking lot to the lake is $2\frac{1}{4}$ in. Based on the map scale, what is the actual distance in miles?

    F 9 mi

    G 27 mi

    H 36 mi

    J 108 mi

41. **Use the table to make a reasonable estimate of about how many people attended the games during the four weeks.**

    Weekley Attendance at the Javelins Soccer Games

Week	Number of People
1	25,097
2	19,454
3	14,655
4	22,508

    A 8,000 people

    B 80,000 people

    C 800,000 people

    D 8,000,000 people

GO ON

42. The volume of the box is 192 cubic inches. Estimate the length of the edge labeled *x*.

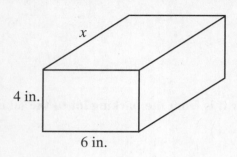

F 8 in.　　　**H** 46 in.

G 17 in.　　　**J** 75 in.

43. Jasmine earned between $30 and $40 a week mowing lawns. She did this for 10 weeks during the summer. What is a reasonable estimate of the total amount she earned?

A $150　　　**C** $250

B $200　　　**D** $350

44. Find the area of the figure below.

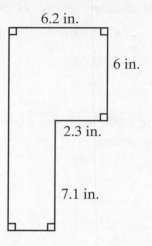

F 27.69 in.^{2}　　　**H** 38.6 in.^{2}

G 37.2 in.^{2}　　　**J** 64.89 in.^{2}

45. Counselors at a day camp decide to take everyone to the movies on a rainy day. Tickets for adults cost $7 each, and tickets for children cost $4 each. The counselors must buy 24 adult tickets. What information do you need to know to find out how much money they will spend in all on tickets?

A The number of tickets they must buy for counselors

B The price of a movie ticket

C The number of tickets they must buy for children

D The amount of money they have to spend

PS SAT 10 Practice Test

46. Sheila records the outdoor temperature every 3 hours. She records the wind rate every 5 hours. If she just recorded both the temperature and the wind rate, in how many hours will she again record both the temperature and the wind rate?

F   5 hours   H   15 hours

G   10 hours   J   30 hours

47. Jamal is a contestant on a game show. He scored well in the first round. His score fell 8 points during the second round, doubled on the third round, and increased by 15 points during the final round. His final score was 107 points. What was his score at the end of the first round?

A   54 points   C   72 points

B   65 points   D   84 points

48. Annie, Darlene, and Thomas have the following hobbies: rock climbing, horseback riding, and bird watching, though not necessarily in that order. Annie is the sister of the bird watcher. Darlene is best friends with the horseback rider and the bird watcher. Match each person with her or his hobby.

F   Annie: horseback rider; Darlene: bird watcher; Thomas: rock climber

G   Annie: rock climber; Darlene: horseback rider; Thomas: bird watcher

H   Annie: horseback rider; Darlene: rock climber; Thomas: bird watcher

J   Annie: bird watcher; Darlene: rock climber; Thomas: horseback rider

49. A siren sounded 26 times to warn people that the ship would be leaving port. Each sounding lasted 2 seconds. Five seconds elapsed between soundings. How long did the entire sounding sequence last?

A   202 seconds   C   150 seconds

B   177 seconds   D   135 seconds

SAT 10 Practice Test

 Mathematics: Procedures

Find each answer. Then mark the space on your answer sheet. If a correct answer is not here, mark the space for NH.

1.
$$\begin{array}{r} 38 \\ \times\ 13 \end{array}$$

   A 51   C 394

   B 294   D 494

   E NH

2. $8 \times \frac{8}{10} =$

   F $5\frac{6}{10}$ H $7\frac{1}{5}$

   G $6\frac{2}{5}$ J $7\frac{7}{10}$

   K NH

3. $9\overline{)648}$

   A 70   C 74

   B 72   D 82

   E NH

4.
$$\begin{array}{r} \frac{5}{6} \\ -\ \frac{1}{3} \end{array}$$

   F $\frac{1}{3}$ H $\frac{2}{3}$

   G $\frac{1}{2}$ J $\frac{4}{3}$

   K NH

5. $12\overline{)1488}$

   A 104   C 124

   B 118   D 224

   E NH

6. $\frac{3}{10} + \frac{2}{3} =$

   F $\frac{29}{30}$ H $\frac{6}{30}$

   G $\frac{5}{13}$ J $\frac{6}{60}$

   K NH

7. $139 \times 478 =$

   A 66,152   C 66,442

   B 66,252   D 66,822

   E NH

8.
$$\begin{array}{r} 5\frac{2}{5} \\ +\ 4\frac{1}{5} \end{array}$$

   F $8\frac{3}{10}$ H $9\frac{3}{5}$

   G $9\frac{2}{5}$ J $9\frac{3}{10}$

   K NH

> GO ON

SAT 10 Practice Test

9. $181.071 \div 33 =$

   A 5.388   **C** 5.691

   B 5.5   **D** 5.790

   E NH

10. $8 - 3\frac{5}{6} =$

   F $30\frac{2}{3}$ **H** $2\frac{2}{23}$

   G 20   **J** $1\frac{2}{3}$

   K NH

11. The workers at Nature's Food Company will send a shipment of 1040 containers of yogurt to a food store. They will pack the yogurt containers in boxes. If each box can hold 12 containers of yogurt, how many boxes will the workers need to ship all of the yogurt?

   A 87 boxes   **C** 79 boxes

   B 84 boxes   **D** 75 boxes

   E NH

12. There are 6 meters of ribbon in the craft basket. How many pieces, each 40 centimeters long, can be cut from the ribbon?

   F 34 pieces   **H** 6 pieces

   G 15 pieces   **J** 5 pieces

   K NH

13. These are Karen's bowling scores for the last five games: 95, 120, 140, 89, 101. Find the mean score.

   A 99   **C** 109

   B 105   **D** 120

   E NH

14. The area below is to be completely surrounded by a fence. How many meters of fencing will be needed in all?

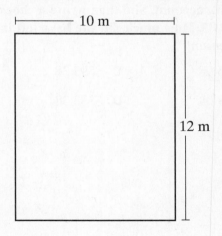

   F 120 m   **H** 42 m

   G 44 m   **J** 39 m

   K NH

> GO ON

15. Mario bought a pair of jeans that were on sale for 25% off the regular price. If the regular price of the jeans was $40, how much money did Mario save?

A $20.00

C $5.00

B $10.00

D $2.50

E NH

16. Carlotta was reviewing the fuel consumption for her car for the past four months. She recorded 23.5, 25.1, 26.1, and 28.6 gallons. What was her total fuel consumption for these months?

F 105.8 gal

H 145.8 gal

G 110.4 gal

J 160.3 gal

K NH

17. Charlene began the week with $456.23 in her bank account. She then wrote a check for $72.85. How much did she have left in her account?

A $435.98

C $393.38

B $398.08

D $383.38

E NH

18. Amy was paid $118.75 for working 12.5 hours. What did Amy make per hour?

F $9.50 per hour

H $8.75 per hour

G $9.25 per hour

J $8.45 per hour

K NH

19. A floor is 8 ft wide. How many floor tiles measuring $\frac{3}{4}$ in. wide each would it take to cover the width of the floor?

A 6 tiles

C 72 tiles

B $10\frac{2}{3}$ tiles

D 128 tiles

E NH

20. Ray ate $\frac{1}{4}$ of a pizza, and Carl ate $\frac{3}{8}$ of the same pizza. What part of the pizza did they eat altogether?

F $\frac{1}{3}$

H $\frac{5}{8}$

G $\frac{1}{2}$

J $\frac{3}{4}$

K NH

◪ SAT 10 Practice Test

21. Mr. Jackson is flying to New York on business. The plane trip takes $5\frac{1}{2}$ h. So far, he has been flying for $1\frac{3}{4}$ h. How much longer is his flight?

A $1\frac{3}{4}$ h   **C** $3\frac{1}{4}$ h

B $2\frac{3}{4}$ h   **D** $3\frac{3}{4}$ h

E NH

22. The price of a share of stock is $10\frac{3}{8}$ dollars today. It was $9\frac{1}{2}$ dollars yesterday. By how much did the price of a share increase?

F $\frac{7}{8}$ **H** $1\frac{7}{8}$

G $1\frac{1}{2}$ **J** $19\frac{7}{8}$

K NH

23. Alex bought 5 granola bars at $0.78 each, 3 containers of yogurt at $1.19 each, and 2 boxes of cereal at $3.89 each. How much did Alex spend?

A $13.25   **C** $15.25

B $15.15   **D** $15.85

E NH

24. At The Food Market, cheese that usually costs $1.12 per lb is on sale for $0.19 less per pound. How much would you spend for 6 lb of cheese?

F $7.86   **H** $5.58

G $6.72   **J** $5.29

K NH

25. A guard walked around a building 100 times. He wants to figure out the distance he walked. The building's base is rectangular. Two sides measure 84 feet, and the other two sides measure 144 feet. How far did he walk?

A 22,800 ft   **C** 91,000 ft

B 45,600 ft   **D** 1,209,600 ft

E NH

26. At Knox Middle School, 120 students play soccer. Of the soccer players, $\frac{2}{3}$ are girls. How many girls play soccer?

F 40 girls   **H** 80 girls

G 60 girls   **J** 100 girls

K NH

▷ **GO ON**

27. Lori wants to save a total of $90 by June. She has already saved $45. What percent of the total has she saved?

   A 20%   C 50%

   B 45%   D 90%

   E NH

28. Which of the following shows the number 382.3782 rounded to the nearest thousandth?

   F 382.379   H 382.378

   G 382.38   J 382

   K NH

29. Use rounding to estimate the sum.
   34.87 + 23.06 + 13.88

   A 66   C 88

   D 72   D 92

   E NH

30. Lynn's mother drove 784 miles on a business trip. The car used 27.2 gallons of fuel. Express the miles per gallon, to the nearest tenth.

   F 27 miles per gallon

   G 28.8 miles per gallon

   H 32.1 miles per gallon

   J 33.2 miles per gallon

   K NH

ITBS Practice Test

Read each question and choose the best answer. Then mark the space on the answer sheet for the answer you have chosen.

1. A fruit snack can be made with one choice of fruit, one choice of yogurt, and one choice of topping. There are 4 kinds of fruit, 2 flavors of yogurt, and toppings of nuts, raisins, or granola. How many different fruit snacks are available?

   A 9　　　　　　C 16

   B 11　　　　　D 24

2. Which of the following numbers is a prime number?

   F 111　　　　H 227

   G 153　　　　J 275

3. Which sentence is not true?

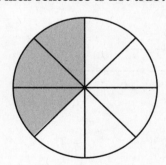

   A $\frac{1}{8} - \frac{1}{8} + \frac{1}{8} = \frac{1}{24}$

   B $1 - \frac{5}{8} = \frac{3}{8}$

   C $\frac{1}{4} + \frac{1}{8} = \frac{3}{8}$

   D $\frac{3}{8} + \frac{5}{8} = 1$

4. Find the elapsed time for a trip that started at 9:15 A.M. and ended at 11:26 P.M.

   F 2 hours 11 minutes

   G 14 hours 11 minutes

   H 12 hours 11 minutes

   J 10 hours 11 minutes

5. Sylvia measured the width of a board to be 7.56 centimeters. How is this decimal written in expanded notation?

   A $7 + \frac{56}{100}$

   B $7 + \frac{5}{10} + \frac{6}{100}$

   C $7 + \frac{50}{10} + \frac{6}{100}$

   D $\frac{7}{10} + \frac{5}{100} + \frac{6}{1,000}$

6. Scott hit the ball 3 out of the 5 times at bat. Which decimal shows Scott's batting average?

   F .350

   G .600

   H .750

   J 1.000

>GO ON

ITBS Practice Test

7. Find the difference.

$$\begin{array}{r} 3.52 \\ -\ 1.05 \\ \hline \end{array}$$

A 1.57

B 2.36

C 2.47

D 3.43

8. A concert stage has the shape of an octagon. How many sides does the stage have?

F 5

G 6

H 8

J 10

9. On a television news show, the weather and sports were allotted 8.5 minutes. If the weather segment lasted 5.8 minutes, how much time was left for sports?

A 2.7 min

B 3.3 min

C 3.7 min

D Not Here

10. Find the difference.

$$\frac{7}{10} - \frac{1}{4}$$

F $\frac{9}{20}$

G $\frac{7}{25}$

H $\frac{9}{10}$

J 1

11. Which of the following angles appears to be a right angle?

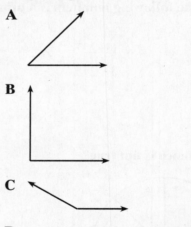

> GO ON

ITBS Practice Test

12. Which of the following is reasonable for the width of a door?

    F 1 cm

    G 1 mm

    H 1 m

    J 10 m

13. A lifeguard swam $\frac{5}{8}$ mile on Saturday and $\frac{4}{8}$ mile on Sunday. How many miles did he swim in all?

    A $\frac{1}{2}$ mi

    B $\frac{9}{16}$ mi

    C $1\frac{1}{8}$ mi

    D $2\frac{7}{8}$ mi

14 If you saved $7.65, how much more would you need to buy a CD for $14.95?

    F $5.30

    G $7.30

    H $9.30

    J Not Here

15. To meet a deadline, a trucker must travel 4,095 miles in 9 days. How many miles should the trucker average per day to meet the deadline?

    A 445 mi

    B 455 mi

    C 475 mi

    D Not Here

16 The two graphs below show the cost comparison between a van and a truck.

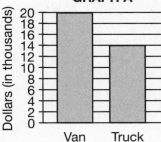

COST COMPARISON GRAPH A

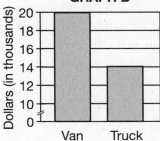

COST COMPARISON GRAPH B

Which of the following is **not** true?

    F The difference between the cost of the van and truck is $6,000.

    G The van costs twice as much as the truck.

    H Graph B might be misleading if you do not read it carefully.

    J The truck costs $14,000.

GO ON

17. Marie hiked 6.71 kilometers on the first day of her outdoor adventure. The trail was 10.4 kilometers in total length. How much farther did Marie need to hike?

A 3.59 km

B 3.69 km

C 3.71 km

D Not Here

18. In a survey, 7 out of 10 teenagers picked rock as their favorite music. How many teenagers out of 80 would you expect to pick rock as their favorite music?

F 17

G 25

H 56

J 80

19. A rectangular soccer field has a length of 100 meters and a width of 65 meters. What is the perimeter of the field?

A 165 m

B 330 m

C 6,500 m

D 13,000 m

20. Add.

$$584 + 487$$

F 961

G 1,017

H 1,061

J 1,071

21. Which expression represents the number of inches in m yards?

A $36 + m$

B $12 + m$

C $12m$

D $36m$

22. Which of the following would be reasonable for the amount of medicine in an eyedropper?

F 10 L

G 1 L

H 100 mL

J 1 mL

23. Find the product.

$$\frac{1}{3} \times \frac{1}{4}$$

A $\frac{1}{12}$

B $\frac{1}{6}$

C $\frac{7}{12}$

D $\frac{3}{4}$

24. How would an 88° angle be classified?

F Right

G Acute

H Obtuse

J Straight

25. The graph shows the dollar amount of sales made at Art's Autos from 1993 to 2003. In which year did sales increase the most from the previous year?

A 1996

B 1997

C 2002

D 2003

GO ON

ITBS Practice Test

26. At a used book sale, Ms. Payne bought *x* books at $1.85 each. Which expression tells how much she spent in all?

F $1.85x$

G $1.85 + x$

H $(1.85 \times 2) + x$

J $x \div 1.85$

27. Find the product.

$$\begin{array}{r} 0.07 \\ \times\ 41 \\ \hline \end{array}$$

A 0.0287

B 0.278

C 2.87

D 28.7

28. Divide.

339 ÷ 3

F 103

G 113

H 123

J 139

29. The population of a town increased from 68,191 to 81,374 in one 10-year period. Which is a reasonable estimate for the increase in population?

A Between 1,000 and 5,000

B Between 5,000 and 10,000

C Between 10,000 and 20,000

D More than 20,000

30. What are the coordinates of point G on the coordinate plane below?

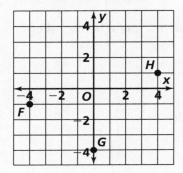

F $(-4, 0)$

G $(0, -4)$

H $(0, 4)$

J $(4, 0)$

GO ON

ITBS Practice Test

31. The table shows a number pattern using dots.

Term	Number of Dots
1	•
2	•• ••
3	••• ••• •••
4	•••• •••• •••• ••••

Which of the following expressions gives the number of dots in the pattern for any term, *t*?

A $4t$

B $t - 4$

C $2t$

D $t \times t$

32. Find the product.

$$12 \times \frac{3}{10}$$

F $1\frac{3}{5}$

G $3\frac{3}{5}$

H $36\frac{1}{10}$

J $36\frac{3}{10}$

33. A pro baseball player had 288 home runs during his 12 years of playing. On the average, how many home runs did he hit per year?

A 22

B 23

C 24

D 25

34. What is the solution of this inequality?

$$d - 12 < 36$$

F $d < 3$

G $d < 24$

H $d < 48$

J $d < 72$

35. On a good day for swimming, the air temperature might be which of the following?

A 0°C

B 10°C

C 15°C

D 30°C

GO ON

ITBS Practice Test

36. Solve.

$$x + 16 = 42$$

F $x = 26$

G $x = 36$

H $x = 58$

J $x = 68$

37. Which is the closest estimate of the product of $5\frac{1}{3}$ and $2\frac{3}{4}$?

A 8

B 10

C 15

D 18

38. The line graph shows the average monthly temperatures in Dallas-Ft. Worth. What is the difference between the highest and lowest average temperatures?

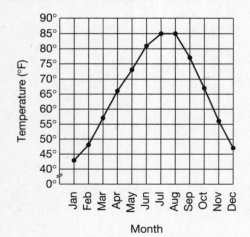

**DALLAS-FT. WORTH
MONTHLY AVERAGE TEMPERATURES**

F 32°   **H** 42°

G 35°   **J** 56°

39. Solve the equation.

$$2x + 3 = 11$$

A $x = 2$

B $x = 4$

C $x = 6$

D $x = 8$

40. For a table cloth, Karen bought a piece of fabric that was $2\frac{2}{3}$ yards long. How many feet long is it?

F 8 ft

G 8.6 ft

H 10 ft

J 12 ft

TerraNova Practice Test

Part 1

Read each question and choose the best answer.
Then mark the space on the answer sheet for
the answer you have chosen.

1 $8 \times \frac{8}{10} =$

A $5\frac{6}{10}$ C $7\frac{1}{5}$

B $6\frac{2}{5}$ D $7\frac{7}{10}$

E None of these

2 $181.071 \div 33 =$

F 6.093   H 5.5

G 5.790   J 5.487

K None of these

3 $\begin{array}{r} 59 \\ \times\ 37 \\ \hline \end{array}$

A 413   C 1,923

B 2,483   D 590

E None of these

4 $2565 \div 15 =$

F 151   H 17 R1

G 170 R1   J 171

K None of these

5 $46.9 \times 12 =$

A 459.8   C 0.5628

B 562.8   D 5628

E None of these

6 $1.001 - 0.36 =$

F 0.965   H 0.631

G 0.975   J 0.641

K None of these

7 $66\frac{1}{8} + 70\frac{3}{4} =$

A $116\frac{1}{4}$

B $136\frac{7}{8}$

C $136\frac{1}{3}$

D $116\frac{7}{8}$

E None of these

8 $45.9 + 6.78 =$

F 1137

G 51.68

H 52.68

J 11.37

K None of these

>GO ON

TerraNova Practice Test

9 Which of these is the best estimate of 308 ÷ 3?

  A 100
  C 10
  B 30
  D 300

10 Mrs. Lee's room has 29 students. Each student received a 4-ounce piece of cake on Valentine's Day. How many pounds of cake did Mrs. Lee serve?

  F 6 lb
  G 7.4 lb
  H $7\frac{1}{4}$ lb
  J 7 lb

11 What is the average of 10, 11, and 6?

  A 9
  B 27
  C 8
  D 10

12 Camille and her 3 teammates ran a 1500-meter relay in 5.564 minutes. What was the average running time for each team member?

  F 1.855 min
  G 22.256 min
  H 1.116 min
  J 1.391 min

13 Which of the following is equivalent to $\frac{34}{7}$?

  A 5
  B $4\frac{6}{7}$
  C $4\frac{2}{7}$
  D $\frac{6}{7}$

14 Which of the following does NOT describe 0.56?

  F $\frac{560}{1000}$ **H** $\frac{56}{100}$
  G 56%   **J** 56:44

15 At her family's garage sale, Bea sold a jacket for $9.75, 2 hats for $1.25 each, and 5 shirts for $3 each. How much did these clothes sell for in all?

  A $14
  B $15.25
  C $27.25
  D $26

16 Which models the ratio 5:3 of circles to squares?

  F ○ ○ ○ □ □
  G ○ ○ ○ □ □ □ □ □
  H □ □ □ ○ ○ ○
  J ○ ○ ○ ○ ○ □ □ □

STOP

Name_____ Class_____ Date_____

TerraNova Practice Test

Part 2

17 **What is the perimeter of Ben's dog's new play yard?**

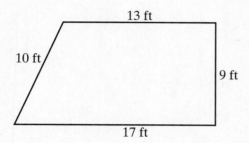

- **A** 59 ft
- **C** 46 ft
- **B** 49 ft
- **D** 37 ft

18 **What is the area of the triangle below? Use this formula: Area = base × height ÷ 2.**

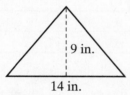

- **F** 140 in^2
- **H** 63 in^2
- **G** 70 in^2
- **J** 17.5 in^2

19 **Leroy traveled 90 miles in 2 hours. Which two rates are equal to Leroy's?**

- **A** 180 mi/3 hr; 135 mi/3 hr
- **B** 180 mi/4 hr; 45 mi/0.5 hr
- **C** 270 mi/3 hr; 45 mi/1 hr
- **D** 180 mi/4 hr; 270 mi/6 hr

20 **50% of 48 is NOT equivalent to which of the following?**

- **F** 0.50 × 48
- **G** 48 × 0.50 ÷ 2
- **H** 24.00
- **J** 100% of 24

21 **Which of the following is NOT equivalent to 0.7?**

- **A** 0.70
- **C** $\frac{7}{10}$
- **B** 70%
- **D** 7%

22 **Ian has 4 dogs. Sylvia has 6 cats. What is the ratio of dogs to cats?**

- **F** 2:3
- **H** 3 to 2
- **G** 6:4
- **J** $\frac{6}{4}$

23 **Sam's father built a wooden form for a cement block. It was $3\frac{1}{2}$ meters long, $2\frac{1}{4}$ meters wide, and 1 meter high. What was the volume of the wooden form?**

- **A** $1\frac{5}{9}$ m
- **C** $7\frac{7}{8}$ m^3
- **B** $\frac{9}{14}$ m^3
- **D** $7\frac{3}{4}$ m^3

GO ON

TerraNova Practice Test

24 Melissa and Eric must have 1,500 worms to start their summer bait business. They will dig 300 worms themselves and buy the rest. The worms cost $2 per hundred. At this rate, how much will Melissa and Eric spend on worms?

- **F** $30
- **G** $24
- **H** $26
- **J** $36

25 Which is the best estimate for $3\frac{1}{5} \times 2\frac{7}{8}$?

- **A** 6
- **C** 10
- **B** $6\frac{7}{40}$
- **D** 9

26 How many milliliters are equal to 3.2 liters? (1 liter = 1,000 milliliters)

- **F** 32 mL
- **G** 320 mL
- **H** 32,000 mL
- **J** 3,200 mL

27 Which of these numbers goes in the box to make the number sentence true?

□ < 4.04

- **A** 4.4
- **B** 4.040
- **C** 40.4
- **D** 4.004

28 Mr. Jay bought 48 apples. He gave an equal number of apples to all of his *s* students. Each student got 2 apples. Which equation models this situation?

- **F** $48s = 2$
- **G** $\frac{s}{2} = 48$
- **H** $48 - s = 2$
- **J** $\frac{48}{s} = 2$

29 Bill needs to use the chart below to hook up 12 telephones. What can he learn from the chart?

Number of Telephones	Number of Wires
1	2
3	6
6	12
9	18
12	

- **A** He needs to use fewer telephones.
- **B** He needs to use longer wires.
- **C** He needs 36 wires.
- **D** He needs 24 wires.

GO ON

TerraNova Practice Test

30 The ice sculptures at the winter carnival were a disaster on Monday. According to the graph, on which day would no melting have occurred?

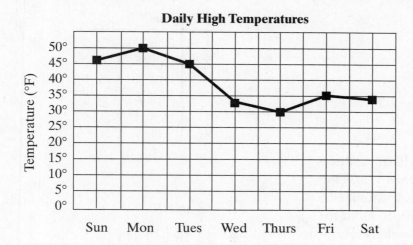

Daily High Temperatures

F Wednesday **G** Thursday **H** Friday **J** Saturday

31 Which expression represents the number of U.S. senators for *s* states?

Number of States (s)	U.S. Senators
25	50
40	80
50	100

A $2 - s$

B $s + 2$

C $2s$

D $\frac{s}{2}$

32 Pepe's dog, Celita, is 1 year old. It is thought that 1 year for a dog is equal to 7 years for a human. How many human years old will Celita be in 9 more years

F 63 years old

G 69 years old

H 70 years old

J 72 years old

33 Which decimal is equal to 8%?

A 0.08

B 0.8

C 8.0

D 0.008

>GO ON>

TerraNova Practice Test

34 To find the number of yards in 18 feet, which of the following should you do?

F Multiply by 12

G Divide by 12

H Multiply by 3

J Divide by 3

35 The Almost Pie apple orchard produces 14,000 bushels of apples each year. The owners pick 3,780 bushels. Customers pick 2,999 bushels. Pickers are hired to pick the rest. How many bushels are picked by the hired pickers?

A 20,779 bushels

B 7,221 bushels

C 13,219 bushels

D 6,779 bushels

36 Which of the following describes the number that goes in the box to make the number sentence true? $10 \times \square = 351$

F More than 40

G Between 3 and 4

H Equal to 30

J Between 30 and 40

37 According to the following stem-and-leaf diagram, what value occurs most often?

Stem	Leaf
4	3 6 7
5	0 1 5 8 8
6	2 2 2 2 4 6
7	3 8 2 4
8	4 4 4 6 1
9	7 3 1 1 1

Key: 4│3 means 43.

A 58 and 91

B 58, 78, and 84

C 84

D 62

38 There are six kittens in the litter. Three are black, two are gray, and the smallest is white. If someone chooses a kitten at random, what is the probability that it will be black?

F $\frac{3}{2}$

G $\frac{3}{3}$

H $\frac{1}{2}$

J $\frac{1}{6}$

TerraNova Practice Test

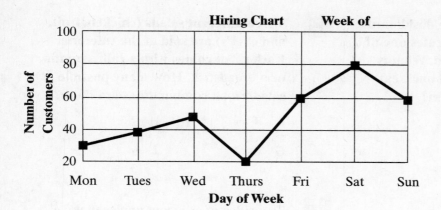

39 Henry needs one server for every ten customers at his café. Use the line graph to determine the total number of servers Henry needs on Saturday and Sunday combined.

A 12

B 14

C 9

D 7

40 What is the range of data values for the graph?

F 100

G 60

H 30

J 20

41 Compare the number of servers needed during the week with the number of servers needed on the weekend. (The weekend includes Friday, Saturday, and Sunday.) Which of the following is true?

A Henry needs the same amount of servers during the week as on the weekend.

B Henry needs fewer servers during the week than on the weekend.

C Henry needs more servers during the week than on the weekend.

D There is not enough information to solve this problem.

TerraNova Practice Test

42 Your car has four doors. The dashboard has a blinking light that indicates one of the doors is not tightly closed. What is the probability that the right backseat passenger door is the problem?

F $\frac{1}{2}$ **H** $\frac{3}{4}$

G $\frac{1}{5}$ **J** $\frac{1}{4}$

43 Twenty-five employees, chosen at random, were asked if they had attended the annual company picnic. Based on the data below, choose the best estimate for the total number who attended if the company has 520 employees?

Attended Picnic?
18 Yes
7 No

A 50

B 150

C 375

D 475

44 Three different salads (chicken, fruit, and chef's) are sold at the cafeteria. Each salad comes with a roll, a muffin, or a breadstick. How many possible salad/bread combinations are there?

F 4   **H** 9

G 8   **J** 6

45 Two sides of adjacent angles make a straight line. If one of the angles is acute, what is the other?

A obtuse   **C** straight

B acute   **D** right

46 Which of the following geometric shapes have 90° and 180° rotational symmetry?

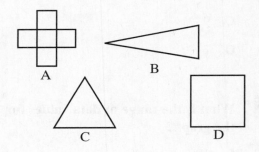

F A and D   **H** B and C

G A and C   **J** C and D

TerraNova Practice Test

47 The school is going to purchase new flooring for the gymnasium. The floor is 80.5 feet by 110 feet. How many square feet of new flooring is needed?

A 190.5 ft^2

B 8,855 ft^2

C 12,100 ft^2

D 6,480 ft^2

48 What is the measure of ∠C?

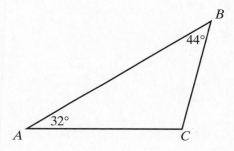

F 14°

G 44°

H 104°

J 114°

49 The rectangular base for a new statue in the town park will be set in 70 cubic feet of concrete. If the length of the base is 5 feet, and the height is 2 feet, what is the width?

A 700 ft

B 10 ft

C 60 ft

D 7 ft

50 Terry described a shape used in a quilt pattern by saying that it is a quadrilateral with exactly two parallel sides. Which shape is she describing?

F parallelogram

G rhombus

H trapezoid

J rectangle

51 Which of the following sets of numbers is in order from greatest to least?

A 7.5, 8.25, 8.6, 8.7

B 8.7, 8.25, 8.6, 7.5

C 8.25, 8.7, 8.6, 7.5

D 8.7, 8.6, 8.25, 7.5

TerraNova Practice Test

52 The number 8 is _____ times as large as the number 0.008.

F 10

G 100

H 1,000

J 10,000

53 What is the rule for this number sequence? 2, 7, 22, 67, 202

A Multiply by 3, then subtract 1

B Multiply by 2, then add 3

C Multiply by 3, then add 1

D Multiply by 2, then subtract 1

54 What will be the next group of dots in the following pattern?

•••••••••••
•••••••••••

••••••••
••••••••

••••••
••••••

••••
••••

F ••
   ••

G •••
   •••

H ••••
   ••••

J •••••
   •••••

55 What value of x makes the equation $4x = 16$ true?

A 4

B 12

C 20

D 64

56 A fish tank is 3 feet long and 2 feet wide. Its height is 1.5 feet. What is the volume of the fish tank?

F 4.5 ft^3

G 9 ft^3

H 18 ft^3

J 12 ft^3

TerraNova Practice Test

Part 3

1 **0.005 + 0.02 =**

A 0.052

B 0.025

C 0.07

D 0.007

E None of these

2 **8.7 + 13 + 2.43 =**

F 12.43

G 24.13

H 23.5

J 23.13

K None of these

3 **693 + 418 =**

A 1111

B 1101

C 1011

D 1001

E None of these

4 **25 × 36 =**

F 900

G 870

H 770

J 225

K None of these

5 **5.324 × 9 =**

A 477.16

B 4.7916

C 4771.6

D 47.916

E None of these

6 **4.3 × 1.5 =**

F 6.45

G 64.5

H 5.8

J 2.58

K None of these

TerraNova Practice Test

7 $1173 \div 23 =$

A 5.1   C 55.1

B 55   D 51

E None of these

8 $4.734 \div 9 =$

F 0.526   H 50.26

G 5.26   J 52.6

K None of these

9 $\frac{2}{9} \times 9 =$

A $18\frac{1}{9}$

B 3

C $2\frac{1}{2}$

D $1\frac{2}{9}$

E None of these

10 $184 \div 13 =$

F 14

G 13 R2

H 15

J 14 R2

K None of these

11 $\frac{7}{9} - \frac{3}{4} =$

A $\frac{2}{5}$

B $\frac{4}{9}$

C $\frac{1}{36}$

D $\frac{2}{9}$

E None of these

12 $11 \times 3\frac{9}{10} =$

F $2\frac{32}{39}$

G $33\frac{9}{10}$

H $\frac{39}{110}$

J $42\frac{9}{10}$

K None of these

13 $385 \div 22 =$

A 17 R11

B 17 R9

C 18

D 17 R1

E None of these

GO ON

TerraNova Practice Test

14 $\frac{3}{10} + \frac{2}{3} =$

    F $\frac{6}{30}$

    G $\frac{5}{13}$

    H $\frac{29}{30}$

    J $1\frac{4}{5}$

    K   None of these

15 $3\frac{6}{7} \times 8\frac{9}{10} =$

    A $26\frac{49}{70}$

    B $27\frac{27}{35}$

    C $31\frac{53}{70}$

    D $34\frac{23}{70}$

    E   None of these

16 $63.254 - 7.9521 =$

    F   66.3021

    G   66.3019

    H   56.3021

    J   55.3019

    K   None of these

17 Write $\frac{7}{8}$ as a percent

    A $12\frac{1}{2}$ %   **C** $87\frac{1}{2}$ %

    B   50%   **D**   90%

    E   None of these

18 $4{,}625 \div 15 =$

    F   36 R5

    G   38 R5

    H   308 R5

    J   380 R5

    K   None of these

19 $418 \times 36 =$

    A   15,048

    B   14,048

    C   3,752

    D   3,762

    E   None of these

20 $30 - 6 \div (1 + 2) =$

    F   26

    G   22

    H   28

    J   8

    K   None of these

STOP

Screening Test Report

Mathematics Concepts	Test Items	Proficient? Yes or No
Number Properties and Operations		
Identify the place value and actual value of digits in whole numbers.	1	
Connect model, number word, or number using various models and representations for whole numbers, fractions, and decimals.	2	
Order or compare whole numbers, decimals, or fractions.	3	
Use benchmarks (well known numbers used as meaningful points for comparison) for whole numbers, decimals, or fractions in contexts (e.g., $\frac{1}{2}$ and .5 may be used as benchmarks for fractions and decimals between 0 and 1.00).	4	
Add and subtract whole numbers.	5, 6	
Add and subtract fractions with like denominators.	7, 8	
Add and subtract decimals through hundredths.	9, 10	
Multiply and divide whole numbers up to three digits by one digit.	11, 12, 13	
Use simple ratios to describe problem situations.	14	
Identify odd and even numbers.	15	
Identify factors of whole numbers.	16	
Apply basic properties of operations.	17	
Measurement		
Identify the attribute that is appropriate to measure in a given situation.	18	
Select or use appropriate measurement instruments such as ruler, meter stick, clock, thermometer, or other scaled instruments.	19	
Solve problems involving perimeter of plane figures, providing the formula as part of the problem.	20	
Solve problems involving area of rectangles, providing the formula as part of the problem.	21	
Select or use appropriate type of unit for the attribute being measured such as length, time, or temperature.	22	
Geometry		
Describe (informally) real-world objects using simple plane figures (e.g., triangles, rectangles, squares and circles) and simple solid figures (e.g., cubes, spheres, and cylinders).	23, 24	
Describe attributes of two- and three-dimensional shapes.	25	
Assemble simple plane shapes to construct a given shape.	26	
Recognize two-dimensional faces of three-dimensional shapes.	27	

Mathematics Concepts	Test Items	Proficient? Yes or No
Data Analysis and Probability		
Interpret pictograms, bar graphs, circle graphs, line graphs, line plots, tables, and tallies.	28, 29	
Read or interpret a single set of data.	28, 29	
Use informal probabilistic thinking to describe chance events (i.e., likely and unlikely, certain and impossible).	30	
Represent the probability of a given outcome.	31	
Algebra		
Recognize, describe, or extend numerical patterns.	32	
Find the value of the unknown in a whole number sentence.	33	
Use letters and symbols to represent an unknown quantity in a simple mathematical expression.	34	
Graph or interpret points with whole number or letter coordinates on grids or in the first quadrant of the coordinate plane.	35	
Express simple mathematical relationships using number sentences	36	

Student Comments: _____

_____

_____

_____

_____

_____

Parent Comments: _____

_____

_____

_____

_____

_____

Teacher Comments: _____

_____

_____

_____

_____

_____

Name_____ Class_____ Date_____

Benchmark Test 1 Report

Mathematics Concepts	NAEP Objective(s)	Test Items	Number Correct	Proficient? Yes or No	Skills Review and Practice
Whole Numbers and Decimals					
Determine whether rounding or compatible numbers is appropriate, and estimate an answer.	N2b	1, 2, 3	□/3		4
Describe whole numbers and decimal numbers using words and symbols.	N1a, b	4, 5, 6	□/3		2
Compare and order whole numbers and decimals.	N1j	7, 8, 9	□/3		3
Recognize properties of addition and multiplication.	N5e	10, 11, 12	□/3		5, 7
Perform computations that involve the order of operations.	N3a	13, 14, 15	□/3		10
Perform addition and subtraction computations with decimals.	N3a	16, 17, 18	□/3		5
Perform multiplication and division computations with decimals.	N3a	19, 20, 21	□/3		7, 8, 9
Data and Graphs					
Calculate, use, and interpret the mean, median, mode, or range of a set of data.	D2a	22, 23, 24	□/3		54
Organize data for use and select a means of communicating data.	D1b	25, 26, 27	□/3		55
Create, use, and interpret bar and line graphs for data analysis.	D1b	28, 29, 30	□/3		57, 58, 60
Describe causes of misleading graphs and statistics, and find an alternative method of solution.	D1d	31, 32, 33	□/3		61

*NAEP (National Assessment of Educational Progress Mathematics Objectives)

N = Number Properties and Operations; M = Measurement; G = Geometry; D = Data Analysis and Probability; A = Algebra

Student Comments:_____

_____

_____

_____

_____

_____

_____

_____

_____

_____

_____

Parent Comments:_____

_____

_____

_____

_____

_____

_____

_____

_____

_____

_____

Teacher Comments:_____

_____

_____

_____

_____

_____

_____

_____

_____

_____

_____

Benchmark Test 2 Report

Mathematics Concepts	NAEP Objective(s)	Test Items	Number Correct	Proficient? Yes or No	Skills Review and Practice
Algebra: Patterns and Variables					
Evaluate algebraic expressions.	A3b	1, 2, 3	$\frac{\Box}{3}$		12
Write algebraic expressions.	A3a	4, 5, 6	$\frac{\Box}{3}$		13
Solve linear equations using addition and subtraction.	A4a	7, 8, 9	$\frac{\Box}{3}$		15, 16
Solve linear equations using multiplication and division.	A4a	10, 11, 12	$\frac{\Box}{3}$		15, 17
Perform computations that involve the distributive property.	N3a	13, 14, 15	$\frac{\Box}{3}$		19
Number Theory and Fractions					
Use divisibility and remainders in problem solving.	N5d	16, 17, 18	$\frac{\Box}{3}$		20
Write or rename rational numbers using exponents.	N1d	19, 20, 21	$\frac{\Box}{3}$		18
Recognize prime numbers and find the prime factorization of integers.	N5b	22, 23, 24	$\frac{\Box}{3}$		21
Solve problems by finding the greatest common factor (GCF) of two numbers.	N5b	25, 26, 27	$\frac{\Box}{3}$		22
Determine the equivalence of fractions.	N3a	28, 29, 30	$\frac{\Box}{3}$		23
Perform computations with mixed numbers and improper fractions.	N3a	31, 32, 33	$\frac{\Box}{3}$		24
Solve problems by finding the least common multiple (LCM) of two numbers.	N3a	34, 35, 36	$\frac{\Box}{3}$		25
Compare the relative values of fractions and decimals.	N1j	37, 38, 39	$\frac{\Box}{3}$		26, 27

*NAEP (National Assessment of Educational Progress Mathematics Objectives)

N = Number Properties and Operations; M = Measurement; G = Geometry; D = Data Analysis and Probability; A = Algebra

Student Comments: _____

_____

_____

_____

_____

_____

_____

_____

Parent Comments: _____

_____

_____

_____

_____

_____

_____

_____

_____

_____

Teacher Comments: _____

_____

_____

_____

_____

_____

_____

_____

_____

_____

Benchmark Test 3 Report

Mathematics Concepts	NAEP Objective(s)	Test Items	Number Correct	Proficient? Yes or No	Skills Review and Practice
Adding and Subtracting Fractions					
Estimate the result of an addition or a subtraction problem.	N2a	1, 2, 3	$\frac{\Box}{3}$		29
Perform addition and subtraction computations involving positive and negative fractions.	N3a	4, 5, 6	$\frac{\Box}{3}$		30, 31
Perform addition and subtraction computations involving positive and negative mixed numbers.	N3a	7, 8, 9	$\frac{\Box}{3}$		32
Perform subtraction computations involving positive and negative mixed numbers.	N3a	10, 11, 12	$\frac{\Box}{3}$		33
Solve algebraic equations involving fractions.	A4c	13, 14, 15	$\frac{\Box}{3}$		34
Multiplying and Dividing Fractions					
Solve problems involving the multiplication of positive and negative fractions.	N3a	16, 17, 18	$\frac{\Box}{3}$		37
Solve problems involving the multiplication of positive and negative mixed numbers.	N3a	19, 20, 21	$\frac{\Box}{3}$		38
Solve problems involving the division of positive and negative mixed numbers.	N3a	22, 23, 24	$\frac{\Box}{3}$		39, 40
Solve problems involving the division of positive and negative fractions.	N3a	25, 26, 27	$\frac{\Box}{3}$		40
Solve equations involving fractions using multiplication.	A4c	28, 29, 30	$\frac{\Box}{3}$		41
Convert measurements within the customary system.	M2b	31, 32, 33	$\frac{\Box}{3}$		43, 44

*NAEP (National Assessment of Educational Progress Mathematics Objectives)

N = Number Properties and Operations; M = Measurement; G = Geometry; D = Data Analysis and Probability; A = Algebra

Student Comments:

Parent Comments:

Teacher Comments:

Benchmark Test 4 Report

Mathematics Concepts	NAEP Objective(s)	Test Items	Number Correct	Proficient? Yes or No	Skills Review and Practice
Ratios, Proportions, and Percents					
Use proportional reasoning to solve problems involving unit rates.	N4c	1, 2, 3	$\frac{\Box}{3}$		45, 46
Use fractions to represent and express ratios and proportions.	N4b	4, 5, 6	$\frac{\Box}{3}$		47
Use appropriate strategies in solving proportions.	N4b	7, 8, 9	$\frac{\Box}{3}$		48
Use proportional reasoning in solving problems involving scale factors.	N4c, M1k	10, 11, 12	$\frac{\Box}{3}$		49
Solve problems involving percents and percent applications.	N4d	13, 14, 15	$\frac{\Box}{3}$		50, 51
Create, use, and interpret circle graphs for data analysis.	D1b	16, 17, 18	$\frac{\Box}{3}$		58
Solve problems involving percents using estimation techniques.	N4d	19, 20, 21	$\frac{\Box}{3}$		52
Tools of Geometry					
Describe and identify points, lines, segments, and rays in various contexts.	G1b	22, 23, 24	$\frac{\Box}{3}$		62
Describe and identify the measurement and properties of various types of angles.	G1c	25, 26, 27	$\frac{\Box}{3}$		63
Describe, identify, and find supplementary, complementary, and straight angles.	G1c	28, 29, 30	$\frac{\Box}{3}$		64
Classify the types and properties of triangles.	G1f, G3f	31, 32, 33	$\frac{\Box}{3}$		65
Classify the types and properties of polygons.	G1f, G3f	34, 35, 36	$\frac{\Box}{3}$		66
Investigate congruent figures and apply congruency relationships to find missing measurements.	G2e	37, 38, 39	$\frac{\Box}{3}$		68

Mathematics Concepts	NAEP Objective(s)	Test Items	Number Correct	Proficient? Yes or No	Skills Review and Practice
Tools of Geometry *(continued)*					
Perform transformations on figures and recognize the effect of a transformation on a figure.	G2c	40, 41, 42	☐/3		70

*NAEP (National Assessment of Educational Progress Mathematics Objectives)

N = Number Properties and Operations; M = Measurement; G = Geometry; D = Data Analysis and Probability; A = Algebra

Student Comments: _____

_____

_____

_____

_____

_____

_____

_____

Parent Comments: _____

_____

_____

_____

_____

_____

_____

_____

_____

Teacher Comments: _____

_____

_____

_____

_____

_____

_____

_____

_____

Name _____ Class _____ Date _____

Benchmark Test 5 Report

Mathematics Concepts	NAEP Objective(s)	Test Items	Number Correct	Proficient? Yes or No	Skills Review and Practice
Geometry and Measurement					
Select or use the appropriate type of metric unit and solve problems involving conversions within the metric system.	M2a, b	1, 2, 3	□/3		71, 72
Solve mathematical or real-world problems involving the perimeter or area of rectangles.	M1c, h	4, 5, 6	□/3		73
Solve mathematical or real-world problems involving the perimeter or area of parallelograms and triangles.	M1h	7, 8, 9	□/3		74
Solve mathematical or real-world problems involving the circumference or area of circles.	M1c, h	10, 11, 12	□/3		75, 76
Use spatial reasoning to identify, define, or describe geometric shapes in three-dimensional space.	G1c	13, 14, 15	□/3		77
Solve mathematical or real-world problems involving the volume or surface area of rectangular solids, cylinders, and prisms.	M1j	16, 17, 18	□/3		78, 79
Exploring Probability					
Determine the sample space for a given situation.	D4e	19, 20, 21	□/3		92
Analyze a situation that involves the probability of an independent event.	D4a	22, 23, 24	□/3		96
Distinguish between experimental and theoretical probability.	D4d	25, 26, 27	□/3		91
Use experimental probability to make predictions about a larger set.	D4j	28, 29, 30	□/3		93

Mathematics Concepts	NAEP Objective(s)	Test Items	Number Correct	Proficient? Yes or No	Skills Review and Practice
Exploring Probability *(continued)*					
Determine the theoretical probability of compound, independent events in familiar contexts.	D4b	31, 32, 33	□/3		
Integers					
Use number lines to describe and compare integers.	N1b	34, 35, 36	□/3		81
To perform addition and subtraction computations with integers.	N3a	37, 38, 39	□/3		82, 83
To perform multiplication and division computations with integers.	N3a	40, 41, 42	□/3		84, 85
Translate between or interpret tables, graphs, and equations representing linear relationships.	A2a	43, 44, 45	□/3		88, 89

*NAEP (National Assessment of Educational Progress Mathematics Objectives)

N = Number Properties and Operations; M = Measurement; G = Geometry; D = Data Analysis and Probability; A = Algebra

Student Comments: _____

_____

_____

_____

_____

_____

Parent Comments: _____

_____

_____

_____

_____

_____

Teacher Comments: _____

_____

_____

_____

_____

_____

_____

NAEP Mathematics Assessment Framework

NUMBER PROPERTIES AND OPERATIONS	TEST ITEMS
1) Number sense	
a) Use place value to model and describe integers and decimals.	
b) Model or describe rational numbers or numerical relationships using number lines and diagrams.	69
d) Write or rename rational functions.	20
e) Recognize, translate between, or apply multiple representations of rational numbers in meaningful contexts.	
f) Express or interpret numbers using scientific notation from real life contexts.	17
g) Find or model absolute value or apply to problem situations.	
i) Order or compare rational numbers using various models and representations.	4
j) Order or compare rational numbers including very large and small integers, and decimals and fractions close to zero.	
2) Estimation	
a) Establish or apply benchmarks for rational numbers and common irrational numbers in contexts.	
b) Make estimates appropriate to a given situation by: identifying when estimation is appropriate, determinating the level of accuracy needed, selecting the appropriate method of estimation, or analyzing the effect of an estimation method on the accuracy of results.	1
c) Verify solutions or determine the reasonableness of results in a variety of situations including calculator and computer results.	
d) Estimate square or cube roots of numbers less than 1,000 between two whole numbers.	2
3) Number operations	
a) Perform computations with rational numbers.	23, 24, 26
d) Describe the effect of multiplying and dividing by numbers.	
e) Provide a mathematical argument to explain operations with two or more fractions.	
f) Interpret rational number operations and the relationship between them.	
g) Solve application problems involving rational numbers and operations using exact answers or estimates as appropriate.	21, 22
4) Ratios and proportional reasoning	
a) Use ratios to describe problem situations.	27
b) Use fractions to represent and express ratios and proportions.	29, 30
c) Use proportional reasoning to model and solve problems.	28, 32, 33
d) Solve problems involving percentages.	34, 35, 36, 37
5) Properties of number and operations	
a) Describe odd and even integers and how they behave under different operations.	
b) Recognize, find, or use factors, multiples, or prime factorization.	19, 67
c) Recognize or use prime and composite numbers to solve problems.	
d) Use divisibility or remainders in problem settings.	18
e) Apply basic properties of operations.	
f) Explain or justify a mathematical concept or relationship.	

MEASUREMENT	TEST ITEMS
1) Measuring physical attributes	
b) Compare objects with respect to length, area, volume, angle measurement, weight, or mass.	48
c) Estimate the size of an object with respect to a given measurement attribute.	
g) Select or use appropriate measurement instrument to determine or create a given length, area, volume, angle, weight, or mass.	25
h) Solve mathematical or real-world problems involving perimeter or area of plane figures such as triangles, rectangles, circles, or composite figures.	49, 50, 51
j) Solve problems involving volume or surface area of rectangular solids, cylinders, prisms, or composite shapes.	53, 66
k) Solve problems involving indirect measurement such as finding the height of a building by comparing its shadow with the height and shadow of a known object.	31
l) Solve problems involving rates such as speed or population density.	
2) Systems of measurement	
a) Select or use appropriate type of unit for the attribute being measured such as length, area, angle, time, or volume.	
b) Solve problems involving conversions within the same measurement system such as conversions involving square inches and square feet.	
c) Estimate the measure of an object in one system given the measure of that object in another system and the approximate conversion factor.	3
d) Determine appropriate size of unit of measurement in problem situation involving such attributes as length, area, or volume.	
e) Determine appropriate accuracy of measurement in problem situations and find the measure to that degree of accuracy.	
f) Construct or solve problems involving scale drawings.	

GEOMETRY	TEST ITEMS
1) Dimension and shape	
a) Draw or describe a path of shortest length between points to solve problems in context.	
b) Identify a geometric object given written description of its properties.	42, 46
c) Identify, define, or describe geometric shapes in the plane and in 3-dimensional space given a visual representation.	39, 41
d) Draw or sketch from a written description polygons, circles, or semicircles.	
e) Represent or describe a three-dimensional situation in a two-dimensional drawing using perspective.	
f) Demonstrate an understanding about the two- and three-dimensional shapes in our world through identifying, drawing, modeling, building, or taking apart.	43
2) Transformation of shapes and preservation of properties	
a) Identify lines of symmetry in plane figures or recognize and classify types of symmetries of plane figures.	
c) Recognize or informally describe the effect of a transformation on two-dimensional geometric shapes.	

GEOMETRY continued	TEST ITEMS
d) Predict results of combining, subdividing, and changing shapes of place figures and solids	
e) Justify relationships of congruence and similarity, and apply these relationships using scaling and proportional reasoning.	
f) For similar figures, identify and use the relationships of conservation of angle and of proportionality of side length and perimeter.	45
3) Relationships between geometric figures	
b) Apply geometric properties and relationships in solving simple problems in two- and three-dimensions.	28, 40, 48
c) Represent problem situations with simple geometric models to solve mathematical or real-world problems.	
d) Use the Pythagorean theorem to solve problems.	52, 70
f) Describe or analyze simple properties of, or relationships between, triangles, quadrilaterals, and other polygonal plane figures.	44
g) Describe or analyze properties and relationships of parallel or intersecting lines.	
4) Position and direction	
a) Describe relative positions of points and lines using the geometric ideas of midpoint, points on common line through a common point, parallelism, or perpendicularity.	
b) Describe the intersection of two or more geometric figures in the plane.	
c) Visualize or describe the cross-section of a solid.	
d) Represent geometric figures using rectangular coordinates on a plane.	
5) Mathematical reasoning	
a) Make and test a geometric conjecture about regular polygons.	
DATA ANALYSIS AND PROBABILITY	TEST ITEMS
1) Data representation	
a) Read or interpret data, including interpolating or extrapolating from data.	47, 68
b) Given a set of data, complete a graph and then solve a problem using the data in the graph (circle graphs, histograms, bar graphs, line graphs, scatterplots).	
c) Solve problems by estimating and computing with data from a single set or across sets of data.	
d) Given a graph or a set of data, determine whether information is represented effectively and appropriately (circle graphs, histograms, bar graphs, line graphs, scatterplots).	
e) Compare and contrast the effectiveness of different representations of the same data.	
2) Characteristics of data sets	
a) Calculate, use, or interpret mean, median, mode, or range.	5
b) Describe how mean, median, mode, range, or interquartile ranges relate to the shape of distribution.	6
c) Identify outliers and determine their effect on mean, median, mode, or range.	
d) Using appropriate statistical measures, compare two or more data sets describing the same characteristic for two different populations or subsets of the same population.	

DATA ANALYSIS AND PROBABILITY continued	TEST ITEMS
e) Visually choose the line that best fits given a scatterplot and informally explain the meaning of the line. Use the line to make predictions.	
3) Experiments and samples	
a) Given a sample, identify possible sources of bias in sampling.	
b) Distinguish between a random and non-random sample.	61
d) Evaluate the design of an experiment.	
4) Probability	
a) Analyze a situation that involves probability of an independent event.	
b) Determine the theoretical probability of simple and compound events in familiar contexts.	62
c) Estimate the probability of simple and compound events through experimentation or simulation.	
d) Distinguish between experimental and theoretical probability.	63
e) Determine the sample space for a given situation.	
f) Use a sample space to determine the probability of the possible outcomes of an event.	
g) Represent probability using fractions, decimals, and percents.	
h) Determine the probability of independent and dependent events.	
j) Interpret probabilities within a given context.	
ALGEBRA	**TEST ITEMS**
1) Patterns, relations, and functions	
a) Recognize, describe, or extend numerical and geometric patterns using tables, graphs, words, or symbols.	54, 60
b) Generalize a pattern appearing in a numerical sequence or table or graph using words or symbols.	55
c) Analyze or create patterns, sequences, or linear functions given a rule.	64
e) Identify functions as linear or non-linear or contrast distinguishing properties of function from tables, graphs, or equations.	59
f) Interpret the meaning of slope or intercepts in linear functions.	58, 68
2) Algebraic representations	
a) Translate between different representations of linear expressions using symbols, graphs, tables, diagrams, or written descriptions.	56
b) Analyze or interpret linear relationships expressed in symbols, graphs, tables, diagrams, or written descriptions.	
c) Graph or interpret points that are represented by ordered pairs of numbers on a rectangular coordinate system.	
d) Solve problems involving coordinate pairs on the rectangular coordinate system.	57
e) Make, validate, and justify conclusions and generalizations about linear relationships.	
g) Identify or represent functional relationships in meaningful contexts including proportional, linear, and common non-linear in tables, graphs, words, or symbols.	

ALGEBRA continued	TEST ITEMS
3) Variables, expressions, and operations	
a) Write algebraic expressions, equations, or inequalities to represent the situation.	7, 9, 14
b) Perform basic operations, using appropriate tools, on linear algebraic expressions.	8
4) Equations and inequalities	
a) Solve linear equations or inequalities.	12, 15, 16
b) Interpret "=" as an equivalence between two expressions and use this interpretation to solve problems.	
c) Analyze situations or solve problems using linear equations and inequalities with rational coefficients symbolically or graphically.	10, 11, 13
d) Interpret relationships between symbolic linear expressions and graphs of lines by identifying and computing slope and intercepts.	
e) Use and evaluate common formulas.	

Correlation Chart: Practice Test to the SAT 10 Standards for Grade 6

SAT 10 Standards for Grade 6	Process Clusters	Test Items
MATHEMATICS: PROBLEM SOLVING		
Number Sense and Operations		
Identify the place value of a digit in a whole or decimal number.	Communication and Representation	8, 9, 28
Identify alternative representations of rational numbers.	Communication and Representation	3, 4, 5
Identify and use order of operation rules.	Communication and Representation	20
Translate numerical expressions into appropriate calculator sequences.	Communication and Representation	
Compare and order rational numbers.	Estimation	
Identify alternative representations of rational numbers.	Estimation	
Round whole numbers to a specified place value.	Estimation	
Solve problems using estimation strategies.	Estimation	14, 40, 42
Compare and order rational numbers.	Mathematical Connections	1, 2
Identify and use field properties of addition and multiplication.	Mathematical Connections	
Match pictorial models to fraction names and notation.	Mathematical Connections	
Translate between visual representations, sentences, and symbolic notation.	Mathematical Connections	6, 11, 13
Identify factors or multiples of numbers.	Reasoning and Problem Solving	7
Solve problems using numerical reasoning.	Reasoning and Problem Solving	10, 44
Solve problems using appropriate strategies.	Reasoning and Problem Solving	46, 47, 48
Solve problems using estimations strategies.	Reasoning and Problem Solving	10, 40, 42
Solve problems using nonroutine strategies.	Reasoning and Problem Solving	
Patterns, Relationships, and Algebra		
Solve problems involving patterns.	Mathematical Connections	15, 16, 17, 49
Solve problems using ratio or proportion.	Mathematical Connections	39
Translate problem situations into algebraic equations and expressions.	Mathematical Connections	12
Solve simple algebraic equations.	Reasoning and Problem Solving	31
Data Analysis and Probability		
Read and interpret tables and graphs.	Communication and Representation	22, 23, 24, 25, 26
Read and interpret tables and graphs.	Estimation	
Analyze tables and graphs.	Estimation	
Identify possible outcomes.	Estimation	20, 26
Determine and use measures of central tendency.	Mathematical Connections	21
Read and interpret tables and graphs.	Mathematical Connections	22, 23, 24, 25
Determine combinations and permutations.	Mathematical Connections	18
Identify probabilities of simple events.	Reasoning and Problem Solving	19

SAT 10 Standards for Grade 6	Process Clusters	Test Items
Geometry and Measurement		
Identify geometric transformations.	Mathematical Connections	30
Identify points on a coordinate grid.		33
Solve problems using properties of geometric figures.		27
Solve problems using spatial reasoning.		36
Solve problems involving perimeter or area.		32, 36, 43, 44
Determine measurements indirectly from scale drawings.	Estimation	39
Estimate capacity using customary or metric units.		
Identify appropriate units of measurements.		28, 29, 35, 38
Estimate or measure length using customary or metric units.	Reasoning and Problem Solving	34, 41
Solve problems involving elapsed time.		37, 45
MATHEMATICS: PROCEDURES		
Computation with Whole Numbers		
Addition of whole numbers using symbolic notation.		
Addition of whole numbers in context.		13, 14, 25
Subtraction of whole numbers using symbolic notation.		
Subtraction of whole numbers in context.		
Multiplication of whole numbers using symbolic notation.		1, 7
Multiplication of whole numbers in context.		25
Division of whole numbers using symbolic notation.		3, 5
Division of whole numbers in context.		11, 12, 13
Computation with Decimals		
Addition of decimals using symbolic notation.		29
Addition of decimals in context.		16, 23, 24
Subtraction of decimals using symbolic notation.		
Subtraction of decimals in context.		17, 24
Multiplication of decimals using symbolic notation.		
Multiplication of decimals in context.		15, 23, 24
Division of decimals using symbolic notation.		9
Division of decimals in context.		18, 27, 30
Computation with Fractions		
Addition of fractions using symbolic notation.		6, 8
Addition of fractions in context.		20
Subtraction of fractions using symbolic notation.		4, 10
Subtraction of fractions in context.		21, 22
Multiplication of fractions using symbolic notation.		2
Multiplication of fractions in context.		19, 26

Correlation Chart: Practice Test to the ITBS Standards

ITBS CONCEPT	TEST ITEM(S)
NUMBER PROPERTIES AND OPERATIONS	
Represent numbers	
Apply properties of numbers	2
Classify numbers by divisibility	
Perform operations	
Write numbers in expanded form	5
Write numbers in exponential form	
ALGEBRA	
Use and interpret operational symbols	
Solve equations	36, 39
Solve inequalities	34
Use expressions to model a situation	21, 26
Explore numerical patterns	31
Understand numerical patterns	
GEOMETRY	
Compare geometric figures	24
Identify geometric figures	8
Describe geometric properties	11
Describe geometric patterns	
Apply the concept of perimeter	19
MEASUREMENT	
Measure time	4, 9
Use appropriate units	12, 35, 40
Identify appropriate units	22, 30
PROBABILITY AND STATISTICS	
Apply probability concepts	6, 18
Apply counting rules	1
Understand measures of central tendency	
Understand measures of variability	
ESTIMATION	
Use standard rounding	29, 37
Use order of magnitude	
Use number sense	
PROBLEM SOLVING	
Single-step	33
Multiple-step	
Approaches and procedures	

ITBS CONCEPT	TEST ITEM(S)
DATA INTERPRETATION	
Read amounts and compare quantities	16, 38
Interpret relations and trends	25
ADD AND SUBTRACT WITH WHOLE NUMBERS	
Add with regrouping	20
Subtract with regrouping	
MULTIPLY WITH WHOLE NUMBERS	
Multiply with regrouping	
DIVIDE WITH WHOLE NUMBERS	
Divide without a remainder	15, 28
Divide with a remainder	
ADD WITH FRACTIONS	
Add fractions with the same denominator	3, 13
Add fractions with different denominators	
SUBTRACT WITH FRACTIONS	
Subtract fractions with the same denominator	
Subtract fractions with different denominators	10
MULTIPLY WITH FRACTIONS	
Multiply a fraction with a whole number	32
Multiply two simple fractions	23
ADD WITH DECIMALS	
Add decimals with the same number of decimal places	
Add decimals with different numbers of decimal places	17
SUBTRACT WITH DECIMALS	
Subtract decimals with the same number of decimal places	7, 14
MULTIPLY AND DIVIDE WITH DECIMALS	
Multiply a decimal number and a whole number	27
Multiply two decimals	
Divide decimals with a whole number divisor	

Correlation Chart: Practice Test to TerraNova for Grade 6

TERRANOVA OBJECTIVES FOR GRADE 6	TEST ITEM(S)
PARTS 1 AND 2	
10 Number and Number Relations • Demonstrate an understanding of number, number sense, and number theory by ordering numbers, representing numbers in equivalent forms, identifying relationships, interpreting numbers in real-world situations, and applying number concepts in real-world situations.	13, 14, 16, 20, 21, 22, 27, 33, 51, 52
11 Computation and Numerical Estimation • Demonstrate proficiency in computation procedures, solve real-world computation problems, apply a variety of estimation strategies, and determine reasonableness of results.	1, 2, 3, 4, 5, 6, 7, 8, 9, 12, 15, 25, 32, 35
12 Operation Concepts • Demonstrate an understanding of the properties and relationships of operations, relate mathematical representations to problem situations, and apply operational processes to solve problems	28, 31, 36, 44
13 Measurement • Demonstrate an understanding of measurement systems, units, and tools by describing, calculating, or estimating size, location, and time; by using the concepts of perimeter, area, volume, capacity, weight, and mass; and by identifying appropriate degrees of accuracy. • Solve problems involving principles of measurement, rate, and scale.	10, 17, 18, 23, 26, 34, 47, 49, 56
14 Geometry and Spatial Sense • Demonstrate spatial sense and an understanding of geometry by visualizing and identifying two- and three- dimensional objects, classifying shapes, recognizing symmetry, using transformations, applying geometric formulas, and evaluating properties of geometric figures.	45, 46, 48, 50
15 Data Analysis, Statistics and Probability • Analyze, interpret, and evaluate data in various forms; and apply the concepts and processes of data analysis, statistics, and probability to real-world situations.	11, 30, 37, 38, 39, 40, 41, 42, 43
16 Patterns, Functions, Algebra • Recognize and extend patterns. • Demonstrate an understanding of functional relationships, algebraic processes, variables, and inequality. • Recognize algebraic representations of problem situations and apply algebraic methods to solve real-world problems.	29, 53, 54, 55
17 Problem Solving and Reasoning • Select and apply problem-solving strategies, identify necessary information, use patterns and relationships to evaluate situations, apply inductive and deductive reasoning and spatial and proportional reasoning, and solve a variety of non-routine, real-world problems.	19, 24

TERRANOVA OBJECTIVES FOR GRADE 6	TEST ITEM(S)
PART 3	
43 Add Whole Numbers • Add whole numbers.	3
44 Subtract Whole Numbers • Subtract whole numbers.	
45 Multiply Whole Numbers • Multiply whole numbers.	4, 19
46 Divide Whole Numbers • Divide whole numbers.	7, 10, 13, 18
47 Decimals • Add, subtract, multiply, and divide decimals.	1, 2, 5, 6, 8, 16
48 Fractions • Add, subtract, multiply, and divide fractions.	9, 11, 12, 14, 15
49 Integers • Add, subtract, multiply, and divide integers.	
50 Percents • Solve computational problems involving percents.	17
51 Order of Operations • Solve computational problems involving the standard order of operations.	20
52 Algebraic Operations • Solve computational problems involving exponents, roots, absolute value, and algebraic expressions and equations.	

Answers

Screening Test 1

1. D 2. A 3. C 4. C 5. D 6. A 7. C 8. B 9. C 10. B
11. C 12. B 13. C 14. A 15. C 16. C 17. C 18. B
19. B 20. B 21. B 22. C 23. D 24. B 25. A 26. A
27. D 28. B 29. A 30. A 31. D 32. B 33. A 34. A
35. C 36. C

Benchmark Test 1

1. C 2. H 3. B 4. J 5. C 6. F 7. D 8. H 9. A 10. G
11. C 12. H 13. D 14. G 15. A 16. H 17. D 18. J
19. C 20. J 21. B 22. H 23. B 24. H 25. C 26. J
27. B 28. F 29. D 30. H 31. A 32. G 33. A

Benchmark Test 2

1. B 2. J 3. D 4. H 5. B 6. H 7. C 8. F 9. A 10. F
11. D 12. F 13. C 14. J 15. A 16. J 17. C 18. J
19. D 20. G 21. B 22. H 23. B 24. F 25. D 26. F
27. B 28. G 29. A 30. F 31. D 32. H 33. D 34. H
35. A 36. J 37. B 38. G 39. C

Benchmark Test 3

1. B 2. H 3. B 4. F 5. C 6. G 7. D 8. J 9. A 10. H
11. B 12. G 13. C 14. H 15. D 16. F 17. B 18. H
19. C 20. H 21. C 22. J 23. C 24. J 25. D 26. H
27. A 28. F 29. A 30. H 31. A 32. H 33. B

Benchmark Test 4

1. D 2. G 3. C 4. G 5. C 6. H 7. B 8. H 9. A 10. J
11. B 12. H 13. C 14. G 15. C 16. G 17. B 18. G
19. A 20. J 21. C 22. J 23. D 24. J 25. B 26. H
27. C 28. G 29. D 30. G 31. A 32. H 33. C 34. F
35. D 36. F 37. D 38. F 39. B 40. J 41. A 42. F

Benchmark Test 5

1. A 2. J 3. B 4. G 5. C 6. J 7. D 8. H 9. B 10. G
11. A 12. G 13. B 14. J 15. C 16. H 17. C 18. G
19. A 20. H 21. D 22. J 23. C 24. H 25. D 26. J
27. B 28. H 29. C 30. H 31. A 32. H 33. A 34. G
35. A 36. J 37. B 38. J 39. C 40. F 41. B 42. H
43. C 44. G 45. D

Quarter 1 Test, Form A

1. $0.67; 0.33$ 2. eleven and seventeen thousandths
3. 206,096.04 4. $<$ 5. 19.1 6. 8 7. \$275.06 8a. 1.5 oz
8b. no 9. 0.0412 10. \$3.94 11. 806 12. 123,620 13. 100
14. 11, 13.5 15. 19 16. $4m + 5$ 17. $p - 9$ 18. yes 19. Add
17 to each side of the equation. 20. 48 pounds 21. 3×150
22. $b = 3$ 23. 2.34×10^7 24. Distributive Property 25. 9
26. 42.2 27. 21 28. 17 29. 22 30. 25 31. 15
32. chocolate 33. 90 34. 90 35. 20

Quarter 1 Test, Form B

1. $0.74, 0.26$ 2. three hundred nineteen and five hundredths
3. 90,840.103 4. $>$ 5. 11.44 6. 280 7. \$1,171.11
8a. 2.251 oz 8b. yes 9. 0.068 10. \$3.63 11. 0.51
12. 0.0852 13. 23 14. 5.75, 7 15. 42 16. $6k + 10$
17. $y + 4$ 18. no 19. Subtract 15 from each side of the
equation. 20. 87 pounds 21. $x + 20$ 22. $d = 63$
23. 6.19×10^{-4} 24. Distributive Property 25. 20 26. 30.9
27. 104 28. 3 29. 6 30. 12 31. 10 32. carpool
33. 19.67 34. 20 35. 22

Quarter 1 Test, Form D

1. $0.67; 0.33$ 2. eleven and seventeen thousandths
3. 206,096.04 4. $<$ 5. 19.1 6. 8 7. \$275.06 8a. 1.5 oz
8b. no 9. 100 10. 11, 13.5 11. 19 12. $4m + 5$ 13. $p - 9$
14. Add 17 to each side of the equation. 15. 48 pounds
16. 3×150 17. $b = 3$ 18. 2.34×10^7 19. Distributive
Property 20. 9 21. 42.2 22. 21 23. 17 24. 22 25. 25
26. chocolate 27. 90 28. 20

Quarter 1 Test, Form E

1. $0.74, 0.26$ 2. three hundred nineteen and five hundredths
3. 90,840.103 4. $>$ 5. 11.44 6. 280 7. \$1,171.11
8a. 2.251 oz 8b. yes 9. 23 10. 5.75, 7 11. 42 12. $6k + 10$
13. $y + 4$ 14. Subtract 15 from each side of the equation.
15. 87 pounds 16. $x + 20$ 17. $d = 63$ 18. 6.19×10^{-4}
19. Distributive Property 20. 20 21. 30.9 22. 104 23. 3
24. 6 25. 12 26. carpool 27. 19.67 28. 22

Quarter 2 Test, Form A

1. No, it is not divisible by 9. 2. $2^3 \cdot 3 \cdot 5$ 3. 24 4. They
would be on the same point. 5. $\frac{12}{18}$ 6. $7\frac{2}{6}$ or $7\frac{1}{3}$ 7. 90
8. $3\frac{1}{2}, 3\frac{8}{15}, 3\frac{4}{7}$ 9. $=$ 10. $\frac{27}{100}$ 11. 6.35 12. 6.4 13. 0.4
and 0.8 14. 12 15. 17 16. $\frac{2}{5}$ 17. Change $\frac{1}{2}$ to $\frac{2}{4}$. Then add
the numerators. 18. $10\frac{1}{8}$ mi 19. $21\frac{19}{30}$ mi 20. $\frac{5}{8}$ m
21. Subtract $1\frac{5}{6}$ from both sides. 22. $10\frac{1}{3}$ 23. 1 h 40 min
24. C 25. $2,200 \times \frac{1}{8}$; 275 calories 26. $12\frac{2}{3}$ 27. $\frac{1}{16}$ 28. $6\frac{3}{5}$
29. Convert the mixed numbers into improper fractions. 30. 9
31. $k = \frac{3}{4}$ 32. 8,640 times 33. ounces 34. 23 35. 3 gal 2 qt
36. 2 gal

Answers (continued)

Quarter 2 Test, Form B

1. Yes, it is divisible by 3. **2.** $2^3 \cdot 5 \cdot 7$ **3.** 16 **4.** They would be on the same point. **5.** $\frac{26}{65}$ **6.** $5\frac{2}{10}$ or $5\frac{1}{5}$ **7.** 168 **8.** $5\frac{4}{11}, 5\frac{2}{5}, 5\frac{1}{2}$ **9.** $>$ **10.** $\frac{11}{40}$ **11.** 11.12 **12.** 9.6 **13.** 0.6 and 1.2 **14.** 7 **15.** 12 **16.** $\frac{1}{5}$ **17.** Change $\frac{1}{3}$ to $\frac{2}{6}$. Then add the numerators. **18.** $6\frac{1}{8}$ mi **19.** $21\frac{7}{15}$ **20.** $\frac{3}{8}$ ft **21.** Add $3\frac{1}{4}$ to both sides. **22.** $2\frac{11}{18}$ **23.** 1 h 18 min **24.** B **25.** $2,400 \times \frac{1}{12}$; 200 calories **26.** $46\frac{1}{2}$ **27.** $\frac{1}{24}$ **28.** 28 **29.** Convert the mixed numbers into improper fractions. **30.** $\frac{2}{5}$ **31.** $p = \frac{5}{6}$ **32.** 11,520 breaths **33.** yards **34.** 7 **35.** 7 gal 1 qt **36.** $\frac{1}{2}$ mi

Quarter 2 Test, Form D

1. No, it is not divisible by 9. **2.** $2^3 \cdot 3 \cdot 5$ **3.** 4 **4.** They would be on the same point. **5.** $\frac{12}{18}$ **6.** $7\frac{2}{6}$ or $7\frac{1}{3}$ **7.** 30 **8.** $3\frac{1}{2}, 3\frac{8}{15}, 3\frac{4}{7}$ **9.** $=$ **10.** $\frac{9}{20}$ **11.** 6.35 **12.** 12 **13.** 17 **14.** $\frac{2}{5}$ **15.** Change $\frac{1}{2}$ to $\frac{2}{4}$. Then add the numerators. **16.** $10\frac{1}{8}$ mi **17.** $\frac{5}{8}$ m **18.** Subtract $1\frac{5}{6}$ from both sides. **19.** 1 h 40 min **20.** $2,200 \times \frac{1}{8}$; 275 calories **21.** $12\frac{2}{3}$ **22.** $\frac{1}{16}$ **23.** $6\frac{3}{5}$ **24.** Convert the mixed numbers into improper fractions. **25.** 9 **25.** ounces **27.** 3 gal 2 qt

Quarter 2 Test, Form E

1. Yes, it is divisible by 3. **2.** $2^3 \cdot 5 \cdot 7$ **3.** 6 **4.** They would be on the same point. **5.** $\frac{26}{65}$ **6.** $5\frac{2}{10}$ or $5\frac{1}{5}$ **7.** 56 **8.** $5\frac{4}{11}, 5\frac{2}{5}, 5\frac{1}{2}$ **9.** $>$ **10.** $\frac{9}{25}$ **11.** 11.12 **12.** 7 **13.** 12 **14.** $\frac{1}{5}$ **15.** Change $\frac{1}{3}$ to $\frac{2}{6}$. Then add the numerators. **16.** $6\frac{1}{8}$ mi **17.** $\frac{3}{8}$ ft **18.** Add $3\frac{1}{4}$ to both sides. **19.** 1 h 18 min **20.** $2,400 \times \frac{1}{12}$; 200 calories **21.** $46\frac{1}{2}$ **22.** $\frac{1}{24}$ **23.** 28 **24.** Convert the mixed numbers into improper fractions. **25.** $\frac{2}{5}$ **26.** yards **27.** 7 gal 1 qt

Quarter 3 Test, Form A

1. 9 **2.** 28 **3.** $6:40; 3:20$ **4.** $\frac{16}{25}$; 0.64 **5.** 0.125; 13% **6.** No; $\frac{10}{15} = \frac{2}{3} \neq \frac{2}{5}$ **7.** 16 in. **8.** Brand A is the better buy; Brand A costs \$0.10/oz, while Brand B costs \$0.11/oz. **9.** 40% **10.** segment **11.** B **12.** $\angle EBD$ or $\angle DBA$ **13.** $\angle ABE$ **14.** 48° **15.** at least two **16.** pentagon **17.** side PR **18.** through the center horizontally or vertically; through the diagonal from upper left to lower right or from upper right to lower left **19.** to the right **20.** $=$ **21.** 0.460 km **22.** $h = 2.5$ ft **23.** $A = 48$ in.^{2} **24.** approximately 94.2 ft **25.** 36π ft^2 **26.** a cube **27.** S.A. = 112 cm^2 **28.** $V \approx 543$ cm^3

Quarter 3 Test, Form B

1. 20 **2.** 55% **3.** $6:14; 3:7$ **4.** $\frac{22}{25}$; 0.88 **5.** $0.8\overline{3}$; 83% **6.** No; $\frac{18}{15} = \frac{6}{5} \neq \frac{5}{6}$ **7.** 30 in. **8.** 48 oz; 48 oz for \$2.40 = \$0.05/oz and 32 oz for \$1.92 = \$0.06/oz **9.** 37% **10.** ray **11.** vertex **12.** Sample answer: $\angle DBC$ **13.** CBD **14.** 138° **15.** none **16.** trapezoid **17.** $\angle U$ **18.** from each of the three vertices to the mid-point of the opposite sides **19.** up **20.** $<$ **21.** 0.212 L **22.** $b = 1.5$ m **23.** $A = 24$ in.^{2} **24.** approximately 376.8 ft **25.** 121π m^2 **26.** 8 edges **27.** S.A. = 102 in.^{2} **28.** $V = 697$ in.^{3}

Quarter 3 Test, Form D

1. 9 **2.** 28 **3.** $5:25; 1:5$ **4.** 0.15 **5.** 20% **6.** No; $\frac{10}{15} = \frac{2}{3} \neq \frac{2}{5}$ **7.** 32 in. **8.** Brand A is the better buy; Brand A costs \$0.10/oz, while Brand B costs \$0.11/oz. **9.** 40% **10.** segment **11.** B **12.** $\angle EBD$ or $\angle DBA$ **13.** $\angle ABE$ **14.** 50° **15.** at least two **16.** pentagon **17.** side PR **18.** through the center horizontally or vertically; through the diagonal from upper left to lower right or from upper right to lower left **19.** to the right **20.** 5.8 kilometers **21.** 35 cm^2 **22.** 12.56 in. **23.** $A = 40$ in.^{2} **24.** 314 ft^2 **25.** a cube **26.** S.A. = 112 cm^2 **27.** $V = 549.5$ cm^3

Quarter 3 Test, Form E

1. 20 **2.** 55% **3.** $6:10; 3:5$ **4.** 0.38 **5.** 25% **6.** No; $\frac{12}{15} = \frac{4}{5} \neq \frac{3}{4}$. **7.** 30 in. **8.** 48 oz; 48 oz for \$2.40 = \$0.05/oz and 32 oz for \$1.92 = \$0.06/oz **9.** 37% **10.** ray **11.** vertex **12.** Sample answer: $\angle DBC$ **13.** CBD **14.** 130° **15.** none **16.** trapezoid **17.** $\angle U$ **18.** from each of the three vertices to the mid-point of the opposite sides **19.** up **20.** 2.1 L **21.** 40 cm^2 **22.** 25.12 in. **23.** $A = 24$ in.^{2} **24.** 28.26 m^2 **25.** 8 edges **26.** S.A. = 102 in.^{2} **27.** $V = 125.6$ in.^{2}

Quarter 4 Test, Form A

1. 15 **2.** $-9, -6, -1, 1, 3$ **3.** 4 **4.** -35 **5.** -8 **6.** 13 **7.** -24 **8.** $(-2) \cdot (-2)$ **9.** $(-4, 3)$ **10.** $(3, -2)$ **11.** 12°F **12.** 1 **13.** vertical **14.** $(4, -1)$ **15.** trapezoid **16.** 4 **17.** $\frac{4}{9}$ **18.** $\frac{9}{20}$ **19.** $\frac{9}{14}$ **20.** 27 games **21.** $\frac{1}{36}$ **22.** $\frac{1}{16}$ **23.** $\times$ **24.** not independent **25.** $\frac{24}{121}$ **26.** Subtract 5 from both sides; then divide both sides by 2. **27.** $x = 3$ **28.** $p \geq 200$ **29.** $x < 3$ **30.** $n + 6 < 15; n < 9$ **31.** $w \geq 15$ **32.** $\sqrt{30}$ **33.** 17 and 18 **34.** When you simplify, $4 + 3 \neq 5$. **35.** $c = 23.3$

Answers (continued)

Quarter 4 Test, Form B

1. 21 **2.** $-17, -12, 0, 5, 7$ **3.** -6 **4.** -14 **5.** -12 **6.** 15
7. -60 **8.** $\frac{(-30)}{(-5)}$ **9.** $(-3, 0)$ **10.** $(2, -4)$ **11.** $-8°F$ **12.** 2
13. horizontal **14.** $(-3, 4)$ **15.** parallelogram **16.** -1
17. $\frac{6}{19}$ **18.** 0.53 **19.** $\frac{5}{7}$ **20.** 6 shots **21.** $\frac{1}{8}$ **22.** $\frac{3}{125}$
23. $\times$ **24.** independent **25.** $\frac{5}{81}$ **26.** Subtract 11 from both
sides; then multiply both sides by 3. **27.** $h = 2$ **28.** $p \le 50$
29. $x \ge -2$ **30.** $n - 12 \ge 15; n \ge 27$ **31.** $t < 18$ **32.** $\sqrt{20}$
33. 22 and 23 **34.** When you simplify, $6 + 8 \ne 10$. **35.** $c = 26.1$

Quarter 4 Test, Form D

1. 15 **2.** $-9, -6, -1, 1, 3$ **3.** -35 **4.** -8 **5.** -24 **6.** B
7. $(-4, 3)$ **8.** $(3, -2)$ **9.** $12°F$ **10.** 1 **11.** vertical **12.** $(4, -1)$
13. 9 **14.** $\frac{4}{9}$ **15.** $\frac{9}{20}$ **16.** $\frac{9}{14}$ **17.** 27 games **18.** $\frac{1}{36}$
19. not independent **20.** $\frac{24}{121}$ **21.** $x = 3$ **22.** $x < 3$
23. $n + 6 < 15; n < 9$ **24.** $w \ge 15$ **25.** $\sqrt{30}$ **26.** 17 and 18
27. $c = 10$

Quarter 4 Test, Form E

1. 21 **2.** $-17, -12, 0, 5, 7$ **3.** -14 **4.** -12 **5.** -60 **6.** C
7. $(-3, 0)$ **8.** $(2, -4)$ **9.** $-8°F$ **10.** 2 **11.** horizontal
12. $(-3, 4)$ **13.** 1 **14.** $\frac{6}{19}$ **15.** 0.53 **16.** $\frac{5}{7}$ **17.** 6 shots
18. $\frac{1}{8}$ **19.** independent **20.** $\frac{5}{81}$ **21.** $h = 2$ **22.** $x \ge -2$
23. $n - 12 \ge 15; n \ge 27$ **24.** $t < 18$ **25.** $\sqrt{20}$ **26.** 22 and 23
27. 15

Mid-Course Test, Form A

1. 10.046 **2.** $3.99, 4.19, 4.2, 4.299, 4.3$ **3.** 70 **4.** 11.46
5. 6:15 P.M. **6.** Move the decimal point two places to the left.
7. 1 **8.** Start with 5 and multiply by 3 repeatedly. **9.** 15
10. 1.4 **11.** $12 \cdot 3$ does not equal 30. **12.** $2^3 p^5$ **13.** 26
14. $(4 \cdot f) + (4 \cdot 3)$ **15.** $15(10 + 10)$ **16.** odd numbers
17. 300 **18.** 7 and 21 **19.** $\frac{3}{4}$ **20.** $<$ **21.** $\frac{27}{12}$ **22.** 12
23. Tom **24.** Write 0.45 as $\frac{45}{100}$, then simplify; $\frac{9}{20}$ **25.** $22\frac{1}{2}$ in.
26. $\frac{12}{23}$ **27.** $\frac{1}{3}$ **28.** $15\frac{1}{14}$ **29.** $12\frac{3}{10}$ **30.** $n = 10\frac{1}{2}$
31. 1 h 50 min **32.** 28 **33.** 14 in. **34.** $\frac{6}{11}$ **35.** $5; \frac{1}{2}$ ft
36. $b = 1$ **37.** 672 times **38.** ton **39.** 3

40.
41. 16 **42.** 90 **43.** Line graph; a line graph shows changes in data over time. **44.** $683 **45.** B3 + C3 = D3 **46.** mean

Mid-Course Test, Form B

1. 106.08 **2.** $6.09, 6.1, 6.2, 6.59, 6.6$ **3.** 125 **4.** 23.42
5. 12:45 P.M. **6.** Move the decimal point two places to the right.
7. 3 **8.** Start with 10 and add 20 repeatedly. **9.** 51 **10.** 1.1
11. 15 divided by 3 does not equal 6. **12.** $3^4 k^2$ **13.** 14 **14.** $(7 \cdot 3)$
$+ (m \cdot 3)$ **15.** $45(10 + 2)$ **16.** It ends in 0 or 5. **17.** 378
18. 9 and 27 **19.** $\frac{1}{6}$ **20.** $>$ **21.** $\frac{21}{6}$ **22.** 6 **23.** John
24. Write 0.32 as $\frac{32}{100}$, then simplify; $\frac{8}{25}$ **25.** 17 in. **26.** $\frac{18}{25}$ **27.** $\frac{13}{16}$
28. $21\frac{7}{12}$ **29.** $8\frac{1}{3}$ **30.** $n = 21\frac{1}{8}$ **31.** 55 min **32.** 33 **33.** 20 in.
34. $\frac{4}{15}$ **35.** $6; \frac{1}{2}$ ft **36.** $d = 1$ **37.** 203 times **38.** yards **39.** 6

40.
41. 20 **42.** 85 **43.** Line graph; a line graph shows changes in data over time. **44.** $241 **45.** B3 + C3 = D3 **46.** median

Mid-Course Test, Form D

1. 10.046 **2.** $3.99, 4.19, 4.2, 4.299, 4.3$ **3.** 70 **4.** 11.46 **5.** Move
the decimal point two places to the left. **6.** 1 **7.** Start with 5
and multiply by 3 repeatedly. **8.** 15 **9.** 1.4 **10.** $x = 2.5$
11. $2^3 p^5$ **12.** 26 **13.** $(4 \cdot f) + (4 \cdot 3)$ **14.** odd numbers
15. 300 **16.** 7 and 21 **17.** $\frac{3}{4}$ **18.** $\frac{27}{12}$ **19.** 12 **20.** Tom
21. Write 0.45 as $\frac{45}{100}$, then simplify; $\frac{9}{20}$ **22.** $22\frac{1}{2}$ in. **23.** $\frac{12}{23}$
24. $\frac{7}{12}$ **25.** $15\frac{1}{14}$ **26.** $12\frac{3}{10}$ **27.** $n = 10\frac{1}{2}$ **28.** 1 h 50 min
29. 14 in. **30.** $\frac{6}{11}$ **31.** $b = 1$ **32.** 672 times **33.** ton **34.** 3
35.
36. 16 **37.** 90 **38.** Line graph; a line graph shows changes in data over time. **39.** $683 **40.** B3 + C3 = D3 **41.** mean

Mid-Course Test, Form E

1. 106.08 **2.** $6.09, 6.1, 6.2, 6.59, 6.6$ **3.** 125 **4.** 23.42 **5.** Move
the decimal point two places to the right. **6.** 3 **7.** Start with
10 and add 20 repeatedly. **8.** 51 **9.** 1.1 **10.** $p = 3.2$
11. $3^4 k^2$ **12.** 14 **13.** $(7 \cdot 3) + (m \cdot 3)$ **14.** It ends in 0 or 5.
15. 378 **16.** 9 and 27 **17.** $\frac{1}{6}$ **18.** $\frac{21}{6}$ **19.** 6 **20.** John
21. Write 0.32 as $\frac{32}{100}$, then simplify; $\frac{8}{25}$ **22.** 17 **23.** $\frac{18}{25}$
24. $\frac{13}{16}$ **25.** $21\frac{7}{12}$ **26.** $8\frac{1}{3}$ **27.** $n = 6\frac{1}{8}$ **28.** 55 min **29.** 20 in.
30. $\frac{4}{15}$ **31.** $d = 1$ **32.** 203 times **33.** yards **34.** 6
35.
36. 20 **37.** 85 **38.** Line graph; a line graph shows changes in data over time. **39.** $241 **40.** B3 + C3 = D3 **41.** median

Answers (continued)

Final Test, Form A

1. 6 hundredths **2.** 170.37 **3.** Commutative Property of Addition **4.** 80.05 **5.** $258.75 **6.** 4 **7.** twelve times m increased by three **8.** $k = 5.6$ **9.** $m = 7$ **10.** 3 **11.** 2 and 8 **12.** 27 **13.** $\frac{9}{11}$ **14.** > **15.** $0.25 - 0.20 = 0.05$ **16.** 7 **17.** $\frac{5}{6}$ **18.** $\frac{3}{16}$ pounds **19.** $x = 3\frac{5}{9}$ **20.** 8:35 P.M. **21.** $\frac{10}{27}$ **22.** $\frac{1}{2} \div \frac{3}{2}$ **23.** $r = \frac{1}{5}$ **24.** 18 ft 6 in. **25.** < **26.** 3 : 4 **27.** 7.5 cups **28.** $0.45; \frac{9}{20}$ **29.** 57.5% **30.** 7.5 **31.** mean, 5.9; median, 6.5; mode, 6.5 **32.** July **33.** 6.5 **34.** 70% **35.** 50% **36.** $\angle PQT$ and $\angle TQS$ **37.** $\angle RQT$ **38.** 7.5 cm **39.** true **40.** 420 L **41.** 12 feet **42.** 35 cm^2 **43.** $C = 27.004$ in.; $A = 58.0586$ in.^{2} **44.** 160 m^3 **45.** −400 ft **46.** −3 **47.** positive **48.** yes **49.** $\frac{1}{3}$ **50.** $\frac{5}{26}$ **51.** 98 days **52.** $\frac{1}{24}$ **53.** $m = 5$ **54.** $k = 9$ **55.** $x > -3$ **56.** $d > 100$ **57.** $b = 9$ **58.** no

Final Test, Form B

1. 2 tenths **2.** 49.5 **3.** Associative Property of Addition **4.** 31.1 **5.** $105.00 **6.** 18 **7.** k divided by three decreased by seven **8.** $p = 8.8$ **9.** $c = 72$ **10.** 5 **11.** 2 and 8 **12.** 33 **13.** $\frac{13}{15}$ **14.** = **15.** 0.25 **16.** 13 **17.** $\frac{1}{2}$ **18.** $\frac{3}{4}$ ounce **19.** $x = 8\frac{1}{8}$ **20.** 7:10 P.M. **21.** $\frac{18}{25}$ **22.** $\frac{3}{7} \div \frac{1}{2}$ **23.** $z = \frac{3}{5}$ **24.** 4 ft 10 in. **25.** > **26.** 7 : 8 **27.** $1.80 **28.** $0.65; \frac{13}{20}$ **29.** 55% **30.** 4.5 **31.** mean, 9; median, 8.4; mode, 7.5 **32.** January **33.** 23.5 in. **34.** 75% **35.** 25% **36.** $\angle PQS$ and $\angle RQS$ **37.** $\angle PQT$ or $\angle TQS$ **38.** 42° **39.** false **40.** 5,300 m **41.** 4.5 m **42.** 27 in.^{2} **43.** $C = 26.376$ cm; $A = 55.3896$ cm^2 **44.** 168 ft^3 **45.** −35°F **46.** −7 **47.** negative **48.** no **49.** $\frac{1}{2}$ **50.** $\frac{21}{26}$ **51.** 8 days **52.** $\frac{1}{12}$ **53.** $n = 9$ **54.** $r = 21$ **55.** $x \le 5$ **56.** $p \le 54$ **57.** $b = 12$ **58.** no

Final Test, Form D

1. 6 hundredths **2.** 170.37 **3.** Commutative Property of Addition **4.** 80.05 **5.** $258.75 **6.** 4 **7.** $k = 5.6$ **8.** $m = 7$ **9.** 3 **10.** 2 and 8 **11.** 27 **12.** > **13.** 0.05 **14.** $\frac{5}{6}$ **15.** $\frac{3}{16}$ pounds **16.** 8:35 P.M. **17.** $\frac{10}{27}$ **18.** $\frac{1}{2} \div \frac{3}{2}$ **19.** $r = \frac{1}{5}$ **20.** 18 ft 6 in. **21.** < **22.** 3 : 4 **23.** 7.5 cups **24.** $0.45; \frac{9}{20}$ **25.** 57.5% **26.** 7.5 **27.** mean, 5.9; median, 6.5; mode, 6.5 **28.** July **29.** 6.5 **30.** 70% **31.** 50% **32.** $\angle PQT$ and $\angle TQS$ **33.** $\angle RQT$ **34.** 7.5 cm **35.** true **36.** 420 L **37.** 12 feet **38.** 35 cm^2 **39.** $C = 31.4$ in.; $A = 78.5$ in.^{2} **40.** 160 m^3 **41.** −400 ft **42.** −3 **43.** positive **44.** yes **45.** $\frac{1}{3}$ **46.** 98 days **47.** $\frac{1}{24}$ **48.** $m = 5$ **49.** $k = 9$ **50.** $x > -3$ **51.** $d > 25$ **52.** $b = 4$

Final Test, Form E

1. 2 tenths **2.** 49.5 **3.** Associative Property of Addition **4.** 31.1 **5.** $105.00 **6.** 18 **7.** $p = 8.8$ **8.** $c = 36$ **9.** 3 **10.** 2, 5, and 8 **11.** 33 **12.** = **13.** 0.25 **14.** $\frac{1}{2}$ **15.** $\frac{3}{4}$ ounce **16.** 7:10 P.M. **17.** $\frac{18}{25}$ **18.** $\frac{3}{7} \div \frac{1}{2}$ **19.** $z = \frac{3}{5}$ **20.** 4 ft 10 in. **21.** > **22.** 7 : 8 **23.** $1.80 **24.** $0.65; \frac{13}{20}$ **25.** 55% **26.** 4.5 **27.** 8.4 **28.** January **29.** 23.5 in. **30.** 75% **31.** 25% **32.** $\angle PQS$ and $\angle RQS$ **33.** $\angle PQT$ or $\angle TQS$ **34.** 42° **35.** false **36.** 5,300 m **37.** 4.5 m **38.** 27 in.^{2} **39.** $C = 31.4$ cm; $A = 78.5$ cm^2 **40.** 168 ft^3 **41.** −35°F **42.** −7 **43.** negative **44.** no **45.** $\frac{1}{2}$ **46.** 8 days **47.** $\frac{1}{12}$ **48.** $n = 9$ **49.** $r = 21$ **50.** $x \le 5$ **51.** $p \le 54$ **52.** $b = 6$

Answers (continued)

Test-Taking Strategies

Writing Gridded Responses
1. 9.32 **2.** 40 **3.** 30 **4.** 2.42 **5.** 1.8 **6.** 464

Answering the Question Asked
1a. C; The question asks for the percent spent on food *and* housing. Add the two percents for these categories. The total is 16% + 32% = 48%, so the correct answer is choice C. **1b.** F **1c.** D **2a.** J; The question asks for the number of boys who participated in a sport other than football. Add the number of boys who participated in all the other sports. The total is 21 + 34 + 16 + 14 = 85 boys, so the correct answer is choice J. **2b.** B

Writing Short Responses
1a. The variable is not defined. **1b.** There is an error in the subtraction. **1c.** $79.82 - t = 74.95$ **1d.** No response, completely incorrect response, or no procedure shown **2.** The method is not shown and there is a subtraction error.

Writing Extended Responses
1. It shows all work and answers to both parts of the problem. The response includes an explanation of why this is the complete answer. **2.** 1 quarter + 3 nickels equals $0.40, not $0.45. **3.** Sample answer: 1 quarter and 2 dimes, 1 quarter and 4 nickels, 3 dimes and 3 nickels; all these add up to $0.45.

Reading for Understanding
1a. the length of the second call **1b.** the beginning and ending times of the call **1c.** 23 minutes **1d.** $1.70 **1e.** $1.15 **1f.** $7.80 **2a.** the pear tree; $\frac{7}{12}$ more bushels **2b.** $5\frac{5}{6}$ bushels

Eliminating Answers
1. Since $1\frac{1}{4}$ is less than the original amount, you can immediately eliminate choice B. $4 \times 3 = 12$, so you can eliminate choice A since it would not take into account the extra $\frac{1}{4}$ cup. 17 is too large since 4×4 is only 16 and $3\frac{1}{4}$ is less than 4. So you can rule out choice D. The correct answer is choice C. **2.** You can eliminate choice J; the numbers are almost twice the original numbers. Since 4 is less than half of 9, you can eliminate choice H. The correct answer must be either choice F or choice G. **3.** Eliminate choice B; since $\frac{4}{5}$ is nearly equal to 1, 50 is too small. Eliminate choice C; $\frac{4}{5}$ is a fraction less than one, and the answer cannot be larger than the original number. The correct answer is choice A or choice D.

Working Backward
1. C **2.** G **3.** D **4.** G **5.** C **6.** F **7.** D **8.** G **9.** B

Drawing a Picture
1. $\angle SQR$ (or $\angle RQS$) and $\angle SQP$ (or $\angle PQS$). Since $\overline{SQ}$ and $\overline{PR}$ are perpendicular segments, the angles formed by their intersection are right angles. **2.** 51 cm²; area of the square = $6 \times 6 = 36$ cm², area of the triangle = $\frac{1}{2}(6)(5) = 15$ cm², and $36 + 15 = 51$. **3.** 32° **4.** 3 **5.** 1 **6.** a square and a rhombus

Measuring to Solve
1. 75° **2.** 120° **3.** 30° **4.** 140°

Interpreting Data
1. C **2.** J **3.** D **4.** F

Using a Variable
1. Let h = the number of horses. $4h = 84; h = 21$; Mr. Drake has 21 horses. **2.** Let t = the amount of tax. $17.99 + t = 19.16; $t = 1.17; the tax on the DVD is $1.17. **3.** Let w = the number of weeks. $18w = 216; w = 12$ weeks; Ed bought gas for 12 weeks. **4.** Let b = the number of boxes. $3b = 342; b = 114$ boxes; Troop 77 sold 114 boxes. **5a.** C **5b.** $r = 11$ rides

Estimating the Answer
1. C; Estimate first. Since the diameter is 1.8 feet, the radius is 0.9 feet. The height is 3.3 feet, which can be rounded to 3 feet. Use 3 for π, 1 for r, and 3 for h in the formula for volume. $V = \pi r^2 h; V \approx 3 \cdot 1 \cdot 3 \approx 9$ ft³. Choice C is closer to the estimate than the other choices. **2.** Estimate using the formula for area of a circle. The diameter of each tablecloth will be $7.8 + 2 = 9.8$ feet, so the radius will be 4.9 feet. Use 5 feet as an estimate. Use 3 for π. $A = \pi r^2; A \approx 3 \cdot 5^2; A \approx 75$ ft²; $75 \times 10 = 750$ ft². She does not have enough material. **3.** J **4.** C **5.** 900 in.³

Answers: NAEP Practice Test

1. C
2. D
3. E
4. C
5. A
6. B
7. D
8. D
9. C
10. C
11. D
12. B
13. E
14. A
15. E
16. B
17. C
18. E
19. B
20. A
21. D
22. C
23. E
24. B
25. C
26. E
27. D
28. B
29. D
30. C
31. B
32. E
33. A
34. C
35. D
36. B
37. C
38. D
39. E
40. C
41. B
42. A
43. C
44. C
45. D
46. C
47. C
48. B

49. D
50. A
51. D
52. C
53. E
54. C
55. B
56. E
57. A
58. B
59. A
60. D
61. C
62. E
63. B
64. Answers may vary. Find the pattern "begin with 3 and add 4 repeatedly" and continue the pattern until you arrive at the 10th term.
65. Check students' work.
66. 15 feet
67. At least 42 sections will be needed to go entirely around the playground. No, neither dimension is evenly divisible by 8 feet.
68. Riverboat
69. Yes; since x and y are both positive, $x < y$ implies that $x \cdot x < x \cdot y$ and $x \cdot y < y \cdot y$, so $x \cdot x < x \cdot y$, or $x^2 < y^2$.
70. $4.50

Answers: SAT 10 Practice Test

Problem Solving

1. B
2. F
3. D
4. J
5. A
6. J
7. C
8. G
9. A
10. G
11. C
12. F
13. D
14. G
15. A
16. J
17. B
18. G
19. C
20. G
21. C
22. H
23. B
24. H
25. B
26. G
27. C
28. G
29. C
30. H
31. C
32. H
33. C
34. G
35. B
36. G
37. B
38. H
39. C
40. G
41. B
42. F
43. D
44. J
45. C
46. H
47. A

48. H
49. B

Procedures

1. D
2. G
3. B
4. G
5. C
6. F
7. C
8. H
9. E
10. K
11. A
12. G
13. C
14. G
15. B
16. K
17. D
18. F
19. D
20. H
21. D
22. F
23. C
24. H
25. B
26. H
27. C
28. H
29. D
30. G

Answers: ITBS Practice Test

1. D
2. H
3. A
4. G
5. B
6. G
7. C
8. H
9. A
10. F
11. B
12. H
13. C
14. G
15. D
16. G
17. B
18. H
19. B
20. J
21. D
22. J
23. A
24. G
25. C
26. F
27. C
28. G
29. C
30. G
31. D
32. G
33. C
34. H
35. D
36. F
37. C
38. H
39. B
40. F

Answers: TerraNova Practice Test

Part 1
1. B
2. J
3. E
4. J
5. B
6. J
7. B
8. H
9. A
10. H
11. A
12. J
13. B
14. J
15. C
16. J

Part 2
17. B
18. H
19. D
20. G
21. D
22. F
23. C
24. G
25. D
26. J
27. D
28. J
29. D
30. G
31. C
32. H
33. A
34. J
35. B
36. J
37. D
38. H
39. B
40. G
41. B
42. J
43. C
44. H
45. A

46. F
47. B
48. H
49. D
50. H
51. D
52. H
53. C
54. F
55. A
56. G

Part 3
1. B
2. G
3. A
4. F
5. D
6. F
7. D
8. F
9. E
10. J
11. C
12. J
13. A
14. H
15. D
16. J
17. C
18. H
19. A
20. H

Answer Sheet

•••

1.	Ⓐ	Ⓑ	Ⓒ	Ⓓ
2.	Ⓕ	Ⓖ	Ⓗ	Ⓙ
3.	Ⓐ	Ⓑ	Ⓒ	Ⓓ
4.	Ⓕ	Ⓖ	Ⓗ	Ⓙ
5.	Ⓐ	Ⓑ	Ⓒ	Ⓓ
6.	Ⓕ	Ⓖ	Ⓗ	Ⓙ
7.	Ⓐ	Ⓑ	Ⓒ	Ⓓ
8.	Ⓕ	Ⓖ	Ⓗ	Ⓙ
9.	Ⓐ	Ⓑ	Ⓒ	Ⓓ
10.	Ⓕ	Ⓖ	Ⓗ	Ⓙ
11.	Ⓐ	Ⓑ	Ⓒ	Ⓓ
12.	Ⓕ	Ⓖ	Ⓗ	Ⓙ
13.	Ⓐ	Ⓑ	Ⓒ	Ⓓ
14.	Ⓕ	Ⓖ	Ⓗ	Ⓙ
15.	Ⓐ	Ⓑ	Ⓒ	Ⓓ
16.	Ⓕ	Ⓖ	Ⓗ	Ⓙ
17.	Ⓐ	Ⓑ	Ⓒ	Ⓓ
18.	Ⓕ	Ⓖ	Ⓗ	Ⓙ
19.	Ⓐ	Ⓑ	Ⓒ	Ⓓ
20.	Ⓕ	Ⓖ	Ⓗ	Ⓙ
21.	Ⓐ	Ⓑ	Ⓒ	Ⓓ
22.	Ⓕ	Ⓖ	Ⓗ	Ⓙ
23.	Ⓐ	Ⓑ	Ⓒ	Ⓓ
24.	Ⓕ	Ⓖ	Ⓗ	Ⓙ
25.	Ⓐ	Ⓑ	Ⓒ	Ⓓ
26.	Ⓕ	Ⓖ	Ⓗ	Ⓙ
27.	Ⓐ	Ⓑ	Ⓒ	Ⓓ
28.	Ⓕ	Ⓖ	Ⓗ	Ⓙ
29.	Ⓐ	Ⓑ	Ⓒ	Ⓓ
30.	Ⓕ	Ⓖ	Ⓗ	Ⓙ
31.	Ⓐ	Ⓑ	Ⓒ	Ⓓ
32.	Ⓕ	Ⓖ	Ⓗ	Ⓙ
33.	Ⓐ	Ⓑ	Ⓒ	Ⓓ
34.	Ⓕ	Ⓖ	Ⓗ	Ⓙ
35.	Ⓐ	Ⓑ	Ⓒ	Ⓓ
36.	Ⓕ	Ⓖ	Ⓗ	Ⓙ
37.	Ⓐ	Ⓑ	Ⓒ	Ⓓ
38.	Ⓕ	Ⓖ	Ⓗ	Ⓙ
39.	Ⓐ	Ⓑ	Ⓒ	Ⓓ
40.	Ⓕ	Ⓖ	Ⓗ	Ⓙ
41.	Ⓐ	Ⓑ	Ⓒ	Ⓓ
42.	Ⓕ	Ⓖ	Ⓗ	Ⓙ
43.	Ⓐ	Ⓑ	Ⓒ	Ⓓ
44.	Ⓕ	Ⓖ	Ⓗ	Ⓙ
45.	Ⓐ	Ⓑ	Ⓒ	Ⓓ
46.	Ⓕ	Ⓖ	Ⓗ	Ⓙ
47.	Ⓐ	Ⓑ	Ⓒ	Ⓓ
48.	Ⓕ	Ⓖ	Ⓗ	Ⓙ
49.	Ⓐ	Ⓑ	Ⓒ	Ⓓ
50.	Ⓕ	Ⓖ	Ⓗ	Ⓙ
51.	Ⓐ	Ⓑ	Ⓒ	Ⓓ
52.	Ⓕ	Ⓖ	Ⓗ	Ⓙ

Blank Grids for Gridded Responses

1.

2.

3.

4.

5.

6.

7.

8.

9.

10.

11.

12.

Student Answer Sheet: NAEP Practice Test

Multiple Choice

1. Ⓐ Ⓑ Ⓒ Ⓓ Ⓔ
2. Ⓐ Ⓑ Ⓒ Ⓓ Ⓔ
3. Ⓐ Ⓑ Ⓒ Ⓓ Ⓔ
4. Ⓐ Ⓑ Ⓒ Ⓓ Ⓔ
5. Ⓐ Ⓑ Ⓒ Ⓓ Ⓔ
6. Ⓐ Ⓑ Ⓒ Ⓓ Ⓔ
7. Ⓐ Ⓑ Ⓒ Ⓓ Ⓔ
8. Ⓐ Ⓑ Ⓒ Ⓓ Ⓔ
9. Ⓐ Ⓑ Ⓒ Ⓓ Ⓔ
10. Ⓐ Ⓑ Ⓒ Ⓓ Ⓔ
11. Ⓐ Ⓑ Ⓒ Ⓓ Ⓔ
12. Ⓐ Ⓑ Ⓒ Ⓓ Ⓔ
13. Ⓐ Ⓑ Ⓒ Ⓓ Ⓔ
14. Ⓐ Ⓑ Ⓒ Ⓓ Ⓔ
15. Ⓐ Ⓑ Ⓒ Ⓓ Ⓔ
16. Ⓐ Ⓑ Ⓒ Ⓓ Ⓔ
17. Ⓐ Ⓑ Ⓒ Ⓓ Ⓔ
18. Ⓐ Ⓑ Ⓒ Ⓓ Ⓔ
19. Ⓐ Ⓑ Ⓒ Ⓓ Ⓔ
20. Ⓐ Ⓑ Ⓒ Ⓓ Ⓔ
21. Ⓐ Ⓑ Ⓒ Ⓓ Ⓔ
22. Ⓐ Ⓑ Ⓒ Ⓓ Ⓔ
23. Ⓐ Ⓑ Ⓒ Ⓓ Ⓔ
24. Ⓐ Ⓑ Ⓒ Ⓓ Ⓔ
25. Ⓐ Ⓑ Ⓒ Ⓓ Ⓔ
26. Ⓐ Ⓑ Ⓒ Ⓓ Ⓔ

27. Ⓐ Ⓑ Ⓒ Ⓓ Ⓔ
28. Ⓐ Ⓑ Ⓒ Ⓓ Ⓔ
29. Ⓐ Ⓑ Ⓒ Ⓓ Ⓔ
30. Ⓐ Ⓑ Ⓒ Ⓓ Ⓔ
31. Ⓐ Ⓑ Ⓒ Ⓓ Ⓔ
32. Ⓐ Ⓑ Ⓒ Ⓓ Ⓔ
33. Ⓐ Ⓑ Ⓒ Ⓓ Ⓔ
34. Ⓐ Ⓑ Ⓒ Ⓓ Ⓔ
35. Ⓐ Ⓑ Ⓒ Ⓓ Ⓔ
36. Ⓐ Ⓑ Ⓒ Ⓓ Ⓔ
37. Ⓐ Ⓑ Ⓒ Ⓓ Ⓔ
38. Ⓐ Ⓑ Ⓒ Ⓓ Ⓔ
39. Ⓐ Ⓑ Ⓒ Ⓓ Ⓔ
40. Ⓐ Ⓑ Ⓒ Ⓓ Ⓔ
41. Ⓐ Ⓑ Ⓒ Ⓓ Ⓔ
42. Ⓐ Ⓑ Ⓒ Ⓓ Ⓔ
43. Ⓐ Ⓑ Ⓒ Ⓓ Ⓔ
44. Ⓐ Ⓑ Ⓒ Ⓓ Ⓔ
45. Ⓐ Ⓑ Ⓒ Ⓓ Ⓔ
46. Ⓐ Ⓑ Ⓒ Ⓓ Ⓔ
47. Ⓐ Ⓑ Ⓒ Ⓓ Ⓔ
48. Ⓐ Ⓑ Ⓒ Ⓓ Ⓔ
49. Ⓐ Ⓑ Ⓒ Ⓓ Ⓔ
50. Ⓐ Ⓑ Ⓒ Ⓓ Ⓔ
51. Ⓐ Ⓑ Ⓒ Ⓓ Ⓔ
52. Ⓐ Ⓑ Ⓒ Ⓓ Ⓔ

Go On

Student Answer Sheet: NAEP Practice Test (continued)

53. Ⓐ   Ⓑ   Ⓒ   Ⓓ   Ⓔ

54. Ⓐ   Ⓑ   Ⓒ   Ⓓ   Ⓔ

55. Ⓐ   Ⓑ   Ⓒ   Ⓓ   Ⓔ

56. Ⓐ   Ⓑ   Ⓒ   Ⓓ   Ⓔ

57. Ⓐ   Ⓑ   Ⓒ   Ⓓ   Ⓔ

58. Ⓐ   Ⓑ   Ⓒ   Ⓓ   Ⓔ

59. Ⓐ   Ⓑ   Ⓒ   Ⓓ   Ⓔ

60. Ⓐ   Ⓑ   Ⓒ   Ⓓ   Ⓔ

61. Ⓐ   Ⓑ   Ⓒ   Ⓓ   Ⓔ

62. Ⓐ   Ⓑ   Ⓒ   Ⓓ   Ⓔ

63. Ⓐ   Ⓑ   Ⓒ   Ⓓ   Ⓔ

Short Constructed Response

64. Short Constructed Response
65. Short Constructed Response
66. Short Constructed Response
67. Short Constructed Response

Extended Constructed Response

68. Extended Constructed Response
69. Extended Constructed Response
70. Extended Constructed Response

Student Answer Sheet: SAT 10 Practice Test

Mathematics: Problem Solving

1. Ⓐ Ⓑ Ⓒ Ⓓ
2. Ⓕ Ⓖ Ⓗ Ⓙ
3. Ⓐ Ⓑ Ⓒ Ⓓ
4. Ⓕ Ⓖ Ⓗ Ⓙ
5. Ⓐ Ⓑ Ⓒ Ⓓ
6. Ⓕ Ⓖ Ⓗ Ⓙ
7. Ⓐ Ⓑ Ⓒ Ⓓ
8. Ⓕ Ⓖ Ⓗ Ⓙ
9. Ⓐ Ⓑ Ⓒ Ⓓ
10. Ⓕ Ⓖ Ⓗ Ⓙ
11. Ⓐ Ⓑ Ⓒ Ⓓ
12. Ⓕ Ⓖ Ⓗ Ⓙ
13. Ⓐ Ⓑ Ⓒ Ⓓ
14. Ⓕ Ⓖ Ⓗ Ⓙ
15. Ⓐ Ⓑ Ⓒ Ⓓ
16. Ⓕ Ⓖ Ⓗ Ⓙ
17. Ⓐ Ⓑ Ⓒ Ⓓ
18. Ⓕ Ⓖ Ⓗ Ⓙ
19. Ⓐ Ⓑ Ⓒ Ⓓ
20. Ⓕ Ⓖ Ⓗ Ⓙ
21. Ⓐ Ⓑ Ⓒ Ⓓ
22. Ⓕ Ⓖ Ⓗ Ⓙ
23. Ⓐ Ⓑ Ⓒ Ⓓ
24. Ⓕ Ⓖ Ⓗ Ⓙ
25. Ⓐ Ⓑ Ⓒ Ⓓ

26. Ⓕ Ⓖ Ⓗ Ⓙ
27. Ⓐ Ⓑ Ⓒ Ⓓ
28. Ⓕ Ⓖ Ⓗ Ⓙ
29. Ⓐ Ⓑ Ⓒ Ⓓ
30. Ⓕ Ⓖ Ⓗ Ⓙ
31. Ⓐ Ⓑ Ⓒ Ⓓ
32. Ⓕ Ⓖ Ⓗ Ⓙ
33. Ⓐ Ⓑ Ⓒ Ⓓ
34. Ⓕ Ⓖ Ⓗ Ⓙ
35. Ⓐ Ⓑ Ⓒ Ⓓ
36. Ⓕ Ⓖ Ⓗ Ⓙ
37. Ⓐ Ⓑ Ⓒ Ⓓ
38. Ⓕ Ⓖ Ⓗ Ⓙ
39. Ⓐ Ⓑ Ⓒ Ⓓ
40. Ⓕ Ⓖ Ⓗ Ⓙ
41. Ⓐ Ⓑ Ⓒ Ⓓ
42. Ⓕ Ⓖ Ⓗ Ⓙ
43. Ⓐ Ⓑ Ⓒ Ⓓ
44. Ⓕ Ⓖ Ⓗ Ⓙ
45. Ⓐ Ⓑ Ⓒ Ⓓ
46. Ⓕ Ⓖ Ⓗ Ⓙ
47. Ⓐ Ⓑ Ⓒ Ⓓ
48. Ⓕ Ⓖ Ⓗ Ⓙ
49. Ⓐ Ⓑ Ⓒ Ⓓ
50. Ⓕ Ⓖ Ⓗ Ⓙ

Go On

Student Answer Sheet: SAT 10 Practice Test (continued)

Mathematics: Procedures

1.	Ⓐ	Ⓑ	Ⓒ	Ⓓ	Ⓔ
2.	Ⓕ	Ⓖ	Ⓗ	Ⓙ	Ⓚ
3.	Ⓐ	Ⓑ	Ⓒ	Ⓓ	Ⓔ
4.	Ⓕ	Ⓖ	Ⓗ	Ⓙ	Ⓚ
5.	Ⓐ	Ⓑ	Ⓒ	Ⓓ	Ⓔ
6.	Ⓕ	Ⓖ	Ⓗ	Ⓙ	Ⓚ
7.	Ⓐ	Ⓑ	Ⓒ	Ⓓ	Ⓔ
8.	Ⓕ	Ⓖ	Ⓗ	Ⓙ	Ⓚ
9.	Ⓐ	Ⓑ	Ⓒ	Ⓓ	Ⓔ
10.	Ⓕ	Ⓖ	Ⓗ	Ⓙ	Ⓚ
11.	Ⓐ	Ⓑ	Ⓒ	Ⓓ	Ⓔ
12.	Ⓕ	Ⓖ	Ⓗ	Ⓙ	Ⓚ
13.	Ⓐ	Ⓑ	Ⓒ	Ⓓ	Ⓔ
14.	Ⓕ	Ⓖ	Ⓗ	Ⓙ	Ⓚ
15.	Ⓐ	Ⓑ	Ⓒ	Ⓓ	Ⓔ

16.	Ⓕ	Ⓖ	Ⓗ	Ⓙ	Ⓚ
17.	Ⓐ	Ⓑ	Ⓒ	Ⓓ	Ⓔ
18.	Ⓕ	Ⓖ	Ⓗ	Ⓙ	Ⓚ
19.	Ⓐ	Ⓑ	Ⓒ	Ⓓ	Ⓔ
20.	Ⓕ	Ⓖ	Ⓗ	Ⓙ	Ⓚ
21.	Ⓐ	Ⓑ	Ⓒ	Ⓓ	Ⓔ
22.	Ⓕ	Ⓖ	Ⓗ	Ⓙ	Ⓚ
23.	Ⓐ	Ⓑ	Ⓒ	Ⓓ	Ⓔ
24.	Ⓕ	Ⓖ	Ⓗ	Ⓙ	Ⓚ
25.	Ⓐ	Ⓑ	Ⓒ	Ⓓ	Ⓔ
26.	Ⓕ	Ⓖ	Ⓗ	Ⓙ	Ⓚ
27.	Ⓐ	Ⓑ	Ⓒ	Ⓓ	Ⓔ
28.	Ⓕ	Ⓖ	Ⓗ	Ⓙ	Ⓚ
29.	Ⓐ	Ⓑ	Ⓒ	Ⓓ	Ⓔ
30.	Ⓕ	Ⓖ	Ⓗ	Ⓙ	Ⓚ

Student Answer Sheet: ITBS Practice Test

Multiple Choice

1.	Ⓐ	Ⓑ	Ⓒ	Ⓓ
2.	Ⓕ	Ⓖ	Ⓗ	Ⓙ
3.	Ⓐ	Ⓑ	Ⓒ	Ⓓ
4.	Ⓕ	Ⓖ	Ⓗ	Ⓙ
5.	Ⓐ	Ⓑ	Ⓒ	Ⓓ
6.	Ⓕ	Ⓖ	Ⓗ	Ⓙ
7.	Ⓐ	Ⓑ	Ⓒ	Ⓓ
8.	Ⓕ	Ⓖ	Ⓗ	Ⓙ
9.	Ⓐ	Ⓑ	Ⓒ	Ⓓ
10.	Ⓕ	Ⓖ	Ⓗ	Ⓙ
11.	Ⓐ	Ⓑ	Ⓒ	Ⓓ
12.	Ⓕ	Ⓖ	Ⓗ	Ⓙ
13.	Ⓐ	Ⓑ	Ⓒ	Ⓓ
14.	Ⓕ	Ⓖ	Ⓗ	Ⓙ
15.	Ⓐ	Ⓑ	Ⓒ	Ⓓ
16.	Ⓕ	Ⓖ	Ⓗ	Ⓙ
17.	Ⓐ	Ⓑ	Ⓒ	Ⓓ
18.	Ⓕ	Ⓖ	Ⓗ	Ⓙ
19.	Ⓐ	Ⓑ	Ⓒ	Ⓓ
20.	Ⓕ	Ⓖ	Ⓗ	Ⓙ

21.	Ⓐ	Ⓑ	Ⓒ	Ⓓ
22.	Ⓕ	Ⓖ	Ⓗ	Ⓙ
23.	Ⓐ	Ⓑ	Ⓒ	Ⓓ
24.	Ⓕ	Ⓖ	Ⓗ	Ⓙ
25.	Ⓐ	Ⓑ	Ⓒ	Ⓓ
26.	Ⓕ	Ⓖ	Ⓗ	Ⓙ
27.	Ⓐ	Ⓑ	Ⓒ	Ⓓ
28.	Ⓕ	Ⓖ	Ⓗ	Ⓙ
29.	Ⓐ	Ⓑ	Ⓒ	Ⓓ
30.	Ⓕ	Ⓖ	Ⓗ	Ⓙ
31.	Ⓐ	Ⓑ	Ⓒ	Ⓓ
32.	Ⓕ	Ⓖ	Ⓗ	Ⓙ
33.	Ⓐ	Ⓑ	Ⓒ	Ⓓ
34.	Ⓕ	Ⓖ	Ⓗ	Ⓙ
35.	Ⓐ	Ⓑ	Ⓒ	Ⓓ
36.	Ⓕ	Ⓖ	Ⓗ	Ⓙ
37.	Ⓐ	Ⓑ	Ⓒ	Ⓓ
38.	Ⓕ	Ⓖ	Ⓗ	Ⓙ
39.	Ⓐ	Ⓑ	Ⓒ	Ⓓ
40.	Ⓕ	Ⓖ	Ⓗ	Ⓙ

Student Answer Sheet: TerraNova Practice Test

Part 1

1. Ⓐ Ⓑ Ⓒ Ⓓ Ⓔ
2. Ⓕ Ⓖ Ⓗ Ⓙ Ⓚ
3. Ⓐ Ⓑ Ⓒ Ⓓ Ⓔ
4. Ⓕ Ⓖ Ⓗ Ⓙ Ⓚ
5. Ⓐ Ⓑ Ⓒ Ⓓ Ⓔ
6. Ⓕ Ⓖ Ⓗ Ⓙ Ⓚ
7. Ⓐ Ⓑ Ⓒ Ⓓ Ⓔ
8. Ⓕ Ⓖ Ⓗ Ⓙ
9. Ⓐ Ⓑ Ⓒ Ⓓ
10. Ⓕ Ⓖ Ⓗ Ⓙ
11. Ⓐ Ⓑ Ⓒ Ⓓ
12. Ⓕ Ⓖ Ⓗ Ⓙ
13. Ⓐ Ⓑ Ⓒ Ⓓ
14. Ⓕ Ⓖ Ⓗ Ⓙ
15. Ⓐ Ⓑ Ⓒ Ⓓ
16. Ⓕ Ⓖ Ⓗ Ⓙ
17. Ⓐ Ⓑ Ⓒ Ⓓ

Part 2

18. Ⓕ Ⓖ Ⓗ Ⓙ
19. Ⓐ Ⓑ Ⓒ Ⓓ
20. Ⓕ Ⓖ Ⓗ Ⓙ
21. Ⓐ Ⓑ Ⓒ Ⓓ
22. Ⓕ Ⓖ Ⓗ Ⓙ
23. Ⓐ Ⓑ Ⓒ Ⓓ
24. Ⓕ Ⓖ Ⓗ Ⓙ
25. Ⓐ Ⓑ Ⓒ Ⓓ
26. Ⓕ Ⓖ Ⓗ Ⓙ
27. Ⓐ Ⓑ Ⓒ Ⓓ
28. Ⓕ Ⓖ Ⓗ Ⓙ

29. Ⓐ Ⓑ Ⓒ Ⓓ
30. Ⓕ Ⓖ Ⓗ Ⓙ
31. Ⓐ Ⓑ Ⓒ Ⓓ
32. Ⓕ Ⓖ Ⓗ Ⓙ
33. Ⓐ Ⓑ Ⓒ Ⓓ
34. Ⓕ Ⓖ Ⓗ Ⓙ
35. Ⓐ Ⓑ Ⓒ Ⓓ
36. Ⓕ Ⓖ Ⓗ Ⓙ
37. Ⓐ Ⓑ Ⓒ Ⓓ
38. Ⓕ Ⓖ Ⓗ Ⓙ
39. Ⓐ Ⓑ Ⓒ Ⓓ
40. Ⓕ Ⓖ Ⓗ Ⓙ
41. Ⓐ Ⓑ Ⓒ Ⓓ
42. Ⓕ Ⓖ Ⓗ Ⓙ
43. Ⓐ Ⓑ Ⓒ Ⓓ
44. Ⓕ Ⓖ Ⓗ Ⓙ
45. Ⓐ Ⓑ Ⓒ Ⓓ
46. Ⓕ Ⓖ Ⓗ Ⓙ
47. Ⓐ Ⓑ Ⓒ Ⓓ
48. Ⓕ Ⓖ Ⓗ Ⓙ
49. Ⓐ Ⓑ Ⓒ Ⓓ
50. Ⓕ Ⓖ Ⓗ Ⓙ
51. Ⓐ Ⓑ Ⓒ Ⓓ
52. Ⓕ Ⓖ Ⓗ Ⓙ
53. Ⓐ Ⓑ Ⓒ Ⓓ
54. Ⓕ Ⓖ Ⓗ Ⓙ
55. Ⓐ Ⓑ Ⓒ Ⓓ
56. Ⓕ Ⓖ Ⓗ Ⓙ

Go On

Student Answer Sheet: TerraNova Practice Test
(continued)

Part 3

1. Ⓐ   Ⓑ   Ⓒ   Ⓓ   Ⓔ
2. Ⓕ   Ⓖ   Ⓗ   Ⓙ   Ⓚ
3. Ⓐ   Ⓑ   Ⓒ   Ⓓ   Ⓔ
4. Ⓕ   Ⓖ   Ⓗ   Ⓙ   Ⓚ
5. Ⓐ   Ⓑ   Ⓒ   Ⓓ   Ⓔ
6. Ⓕ   Ⓖ   Ⓗ   Ⓙ   Ⓚ
7. Ⓐ   Ⓑ   Ⓒ   Ⓓ   Ⓔ
8. Ⓕ   Ⓖ   Ⓗ   Ⓙ   Ⓚ
9. Ⓐ   Ⓑ   Ⓒ   Ⓓ   Ⓔ
10. Ⓕ   Ⓖ   Ⓗ   Ⓙ   Ⓚ
11. Ⓐ   Ⓑ   Ⓒ   Ⓓ   Ⓔ
12. Ⓕ   Ⓖ   Ⓗ   Ⓙ   Ⓚ
13. Ⓐ   Ⓑ   Ⓒ   Ⓓ   Ⓔ
14. Ⓕ   Ⓖ   Ⓗ   Ⓙ   Ⓚ
15. Ⓐ   Ⓑ   Ⓒ   Ⓓ   Ⓔ
16. Ⓕ   Ⓖ   Ⓗ   Ⓙ   Ⓚ
17. Ⓐ   Ⓑ   Ⓒ   Ⓓ   Ⓔ
18. Ⓕ   Ⓖ   Ⓗ   Ⓙ   Ⓚ
19. Ⓐ   Ⓑ   Ⓒ   Ⓓ   Ⓔ
20. Ⓕ   Ⓖ   Ⓗ   Ⓙ   Ⓚ